"Danna has written a very practical 40-day devotional that teaches women to change and adjust to biblical thinking. I know both of us would say to make sure that no devotional—no book—keeps you from studying God's book, the Bible, for yourself."

Kay Arthur, Co-CEO, Precept Ministries International

"If you are sad, discouraged, disappointed, bored, hopeless, numb, angry, or drowning in the sea of the torrential storms of life, Danna and her wise friends can guide you to a better place where the sun does shine, and you can bask in the warmth of God's love, protection, and life-giving hope. Day by day, you will discover the life you so long for. What happened to your life? You just found it within the pages of this book."

Pam Farrel, author of over 30 books, including *Men Are Like Waffles, Women Are Like Spaghetti, The 10 Best Decisions a Woman Can Make,* and *Woman of Confidence*

What happened *to my* life?

Finding New Passion, Purpose, and Joy

DANNA DEMETRE

Revell
a division of Baker Publishing Group
Grand Rapids, Michigan

Published by Revell
a division of Baker Publishing Group
P.O. Box 6287, Grand Rapids, MI 49516-6287
www.revellbooks.com

Printed in the United States of America

Library of Congress Cataloging-in-Publication Data
Demetre, Danna.
    What happened to my life? : finding new passion, purpose, and joy / Danna
Demetre.
       p. cm.
    Includes bibliographical references.
    ISBN 978-0-8007-3352-0 (pbk.)
    1. Christian women—Religious life. 2. Christian life. 3. Contentment—Religious aspects—Christianity. I. Title.
BV4527.D45 2010
248.8′43—dc22   2010001467

Published in association with the literary agency of Alive Communications, Inc., 7680 Goddard Street, Suite 200, Colorado Springs, Colorado 80920. www.alivecommunications.com.

10   11   12   13   14   15   16   7   6   5   4   3   2   1

To Lew, my husband of twenty-five years,

You are the love of my life, my friend for eternity. You and I have had our ups and downs. In 1984, I gave you a cross to wear with an inscription that read: Forever, D 1984. Forever seemed like way too long in our difficult years. Today, to know that I will spend eternity with my best friend is a great source of comfort and joy. God has been faithful to show us that no matter how challenging life can get, he will see us through. Thank you for being a consistent encourager in my ministry even when I had doubts. Thank you for being my source of strength when I was weak or tired. Second only to Christ, you have stood by me in the best of times . . . and in the worst. I am so thankful we are now living in the best. What happened to my life can only be explained as being touched by the grace of God!

Forever,

D
2009

Contents

Acknowledgments

The subject of this book has become very near and dear to my heart as I have spoken around the country and met women in their various struggles. They love God and yet wonder, "What happened to my life? What is wrong with me? Why can't I be content when I am a child of the King?" This journey of life on our fallen planet is hard. I am so thankful that my publisher, Revell, is willing to let me take on this project and publish my fourth book with them.

I owe a special thanks to Jennifer Leep for believing in me and promoting my ideas to her team at Revell since 2000. I still feel like the new kid on the block and am in awe each time I see a new book with my name on it hit the shelves.

Beth Jusino, my literary agent with Alive Communications, has been a great source of encouragement and direction. She's always available and gracious despite the first time I met her; I blew right by her, not realizing she was *my* agent! Oops! Beth, you're so good at what you do.

Special thanks are in order for the women who were willing to share their personal stories within these pages. They have lived through some tough circumstances and have learned the secret of contentment that the apostle Paul speaks about.

Mary, you are as beautiful inside as you are outside. Your amazing voice sings of God's incredible transformation of your life.

Sylvia, my "Jonathan" in this life, you are a friend of the heart that sticks closer than a "sister." We've been through a lot, and I love you immensely. When I get to heaven, I want to sing like you!

Kris, your wonderful sense of humor is the first thing that comes to my mind when I think about you. And then I remember your deep love for Christ and know that you live out the verse, "The joy of the LORD is your strength" (Neh. 8:10).

Kimberly, God has given you such a resilient heart. Your years walking with the Lord created great faith, which carried you with grace through the darkest hours. You are truly the perfect mom. I know I'm much older than you, but I wish you could have been my model.

Diana, smart, witty, and deep are just a few of the words that describe you. The Word of God abides in you deeply and guides you wisely. I am honored to call you friend.

Marilyn, the joy of the Lord is your strength. You have endured a childhood that makes us shudder and yet God has not only sustained you but caused you to flourish as a confident woman and leader. Your testimony of transformation is an inspiration to us all.

Jesus Christ, you are the only reason that I live and breathe and have my being. Thank you for dying for my sins and setting me free. You have given me all I need to be content and live with passion, purpose, and joy.

Introduction

Is This Book for You?

If you are discontent with your life today . . . this book is for you.

If you are bored, angry, or frustrated . . . this book is for you.

If you are stressed-out and running like a hamster in a wheel . . . this book is for you.

If you are unhappy, but don't know why . . . this book is for you.

If you are discouraged because life isn't fair . . . this book is for you.

If you have had more heartbreak than one woman can handle . . . this book is for you.

If you have created more heartbreak than one woman should . . . this book is for you.

If you are living in mediocre complacency . . . this book is for you.

If you cannot find joy and purpose most days despite your circumstances . . . this book is for you.

Have you ever had a day, a month, or even a year when you hated your life? Perhaps you just came to the end of yourself and wondered, what happened to my life? If so, this book is for you.

Whether you are dealing with a life crisis or simply feeling that your existence is not at all what you had hoped it would be, this book will help you learn how to find authentic contentment and joy despite your circumstances. It will help move you from simply surviving to truly thriving once again.

For many women, busyness is one of the key factors in a life that lacks joy. The tyranny of the urgent too often drowns out the importance of life's fragile essentials. I know because I was once an aspiring superwoman, believing I could do it all. I learned the hard way that the ultimate cost for living on the edge can be very high.

Whether your issue is busyness, over-the-top life challenges, or simply a discontented heart, you can find life-changing solutions in the Word of God. The Lord is concerned about the details of our lives. He cares how we invest every moment. He is not overly impressed with our accomplishments but rather with our personal transformation and how we affect others.

Now in my late fifties, I've learned and applied some important biblical principles that have brought great peace and balance back to my life. I am still a work in progress, but my husband will tell you (with great relief and joy) how much differently I approach life and how this difference has transformed our family on many levels.

We don't need more courses on time management. We don't need to figure out how to survive on less sleep or how to multitask more efficiently. In truth, most of us simply need to slow down and make better choices. We need to reinterpret life and have more realistic expectations. We need to choose the very best from among all the good and surrender our entire life to God and his purposes. I'm not saying that you need to join a monastery but rather pursue God in a life-changing way.

My husband, son, and I recently lived in breathtaking Lugano, Switzerland, for two years. The language and culture are Italian in this land that I fondly call "Switzaly." The pace is much slower there. Things just don't get done the way they do in the States. And you learn quickly either to let go . . . or go crazy. Letting go is essential to finding balance and joy. When we returned to California this past summer, I decided to be intentional about continuing the pace we lived in Lugano—to linger over candlelit dinners and engage in long, passionate conversations, to stay away from the stores and malls on Sunday, to walk more, to watch less television, and, most importantly, to spend more quiet moments with God.

Whether you are single or married, young or old, living a life of contentment is essential to fulfilling God's perfect plan for your life. I hope and pray you will discover the freedom God has for those who walk according to his purpose in the details of life. In the following pages, you will discover deep yet practical biblical truths that have the power to transform your life profoundly. I know, because they have transformed mine. In my fifty-seven years on this planet, I've experienced a prolonged eating disorder, debilitating panic attacks, infidelity, divorce, a blended family, more infidelity, my child's teen pregnancy, an incarcerated adult child, and more. Some of my challenges were of my own making, while many were out of my control. I'm quite sure there are more adventures in store if God gives me another decade or two of life. And whatever days I have left, I plan to live them with great passion and purpose, as he intended!

So how about you? How many months or years of your gift of life have you squandered by living in emotional or spiritual poverty? Have you been so busy that you've missed many of God's divine appointments? I know how insidious our discontentment can become. It grows like a hidden cancer until it has metastasized to our very soul.

I invite you to join me on a journey to discover the one thing worth pursuing, to implement a few simple yet transforming life habits, and to realize the incredible life God has for those who love him and "have been called according to his purpose" (Rom. 8:28).

My prayer for you is this beautiful passage from Ephesians 3:14–21:

> For this reason I kneel before the Father, from whom his whole family in heaven and on earth derives its name. I pray that out of his glorious riches he may strengthen you with power through his Spirit in your inner being, so that Christ may dwell in your hearts through faith. And I pray that you, being rooted and established in love, may have power, together with all the saints, to grasp how wide and long and high and deep is the love of Christ, and to know this love that surpasses knowledge—that you may be filled to the measure of all the fullness of God. Now to him who is able to do immeasurably more than all we ask or imagine, according to his power that is at work within us, to him be glory in the church and in Christ Jesus throughout all generations, for ever and ever! Amen.

PART 1

what's wrong with me anyway?

Expectations and Your Misery Factor

It's a Wonderful Life

Life couldn't be more perfect . . . in my imagination. I grew up in the fifties and sixties watching syrupy sweet television shows like *Leave It to Beaver*, *Donna Reed*, and *Ozzie and Harriet*. If you are too young to have experienced these, try to find them on a DVD or late-night syndications. You'll crack up watching all the wives doing dishes and vacuuming in their crisp cotton dresses. Most weekly programs revolved around the major challenge of parents teaching their children not to lie and how to get along with others. High school dropouts, drug abuse, and teen pregnancy were not issues we saw addressed on our black-and-white television screens. Life was clean, orderly, and oh so well balanced.

As a result of my preconceived notions, I had a clear picture of what my life should be like at each major stage. I'd marry a handsome professional man, and after a few years of wedded bliss, we'd have two or three beautiful and well-behaved children.

I must admit, though, that I never had any desire to wash dishes in a dress. Besides, in my fantasy we'd be able to afford a housekeeper at least once a week. And last but not least, I'd pursue my career balanced perfectly between my excellent mothering role and my romantic marital priorities.

The Dream Bubble Popped

I sat in the waiting area wondering what went wrong. How could I have made so many bad choices that affected not only my life but also the lives of my children? Just then, my thoughts were interrupted as my daughter Jamie approached. Her dark, thick, curly hair was pulled back in a low ponytail, and her smooth skin was shockingly white except for the dark gray circles under her eyes. Tears started to well up in those deep brown eyes and spilled over onto her cheeks before she could even sit down and pick up the phone behind the glass window that separated us. So close . . . yet so very far away.

Jamie had been busted for trafficking drugs . . . again. This time it was cocaine, not marijuana. This time she faced federal prison time—up to ten years—not forty days in a local women's detention center. Those forty days had scared her. This time she was terrified. Forty days doesn't change one's character. I hoped and prayed that prison time would.

She had screeched at me in anger when I had refused call after call to bail her out. Now she was exhausted, broken, and helpless. Perhaps for the first time in years she was ready to receive some help. I felt like I was playing a role in a bad movie that did not have one of those old-fashioned "happily ever after" endings. I didn't like the script, I didn't like the parts, and I didn't like the set. But one thing I knew for sure was that I loved the Director. Despite my fear and pain, I had enough spiritual grounding to know that God was there with us in this very sad situation. And so I prayed my knees raw, knowing that God might not change the script to my liking but that he did love my daughter and would draw her to him if only she would surrender.

Thankfully, Jamie did pursue the one thing that would not only get her through but would also secure her future for eternity—trusting Jesus Christ as her personal Savior. Her life had been in the gutter before she went to prison. It wasn't until she reached the dark, dirty bottom of the pit that there was only one place to look . . . up. Later, I will share more about God's transforming work in the life of my beautiful daughter.

When the storms of life hit, and they do all too often, we cannot subdue them. But we can hunker down and be prepared to weather them as God gives us strength and wisdom. I believe with all my heart that when we have truth firmly rooted in our hearts and minds, the peace and joy of the Lord puts us in the eye of the storm, where there is calm despite all the chaos going on around us. In the eye, we are safe and secure in our spirits. In the eye, we can endure because we have an eternal perspective, much the way women see the labor that precedes childbirth for what it really is—a means to a wonderful end, a beautiful baby.

The Labor of Life

The analogy of life being like childbirth is used several times in Scripture. In John 16:21–22, Jesus prepares the disciples for his death and helps them deal with their impending grief by telling them, "A woman giving birth to a child has pain because her time has come; but when her baby is born she forgets the anguish because of her joy that a child is born into the world. So with you: Now is your time of grief, but I will see you again and you will rejoice, and no one will take away your joy."

Having been a labor and delivery nurse for thirteen years, I saw my share of deliveries. Never in all those years of teaching childbirth education or coaching women through labor did I once hear a woman say, "I just can't wait for those contractions to start. I just love being in pain." Mothers know that it is a part of the "work" of having children. They may not desire the pain, but they do desire the child. Therefore, many women seek to be educated and coached through the painful process of childbirth, knowing that even the best of anesthesia cannot be administered with the first contraction!

Like all aspects of life, on some occasions the pain produces more pain in the form of a diseased, deformed, or stillborn child. Yet, most women who experience such deep loss return to experience pregnancy and childbirth again, trusting in a more positive outcome. That is because most mothers know that the pain and fear are nothing compared to the reward.

So it is with this life. Life is labor. Life is painful. Our ultimate delivery will be into heaven, where God has stored up all our blessings. On this side, we will have a mix of joy and sorrow. It is our human condition (saved or not). Sadly, too much of our pain is of our own making. We become discontent and unhappy striving for what we passionately want while often ignoring what we really need. That has certainly been my personal challenge.

In recent years, my focus has been to "set my mind on things above," as Paul admonishes us in Colossians 3:2. How about you? Are you struggling in this area as well? If we are to make any real progress in this area, we must be willing to "get real," to relentlessly uncover the lies we believe and replace them with truth. If our desires, goals, and plans are not sifted through the grid of biblical truth, they will often send us down the wrong path.

The Misery Factor

Another important issue impacting our contentment is that our expectations of this life must be in sync with reality. Misunderstanding biblical truth and expecting God to fulfill a promise he never really made can result in both poor decisions and painful consequences.

About a decade ago, I became more serious about my study of the Bible. It seemed the more I studied, the more I began to understand why my misconceptions about God and his Word were creating what our close friend and pastor, Tim Scott, likes to call "the misery factor."[1] He says that the degree that our expectations exceed reality determines the intensity of our misery. In other words, if we base our contentment on the expectation that something must happen for us to have true joy, and that "something" is unrealistic or completely out of our control, our misery factor increases. As illustrated in the graph below, the distance between reality and our expectations determines the level of our misery!

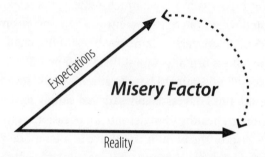

Imagine a mother of two children whose husband has decided to leave her for a younger woman. Not only does he leave her alone to raise their boys, but within a year he also marries his young mistress. If this hurting, rejected woman places all her hopes and dreams for a fulfilled life on getting her ex-husband back, her misery will be great.

I am not saying that miracles don't happen. But if God does not answer those prayers over time, she may miss some of the opportunities he brings her way. For example, he may provide deep friendships with other women who can comfort or mentor her. He may even deliver a godly man when the time is right. If she chooses to receive the incredible healing and love that only God can give her, she opens up her heart and life to new possibilities. But if she maintains unrealistic expectations when it is clear God's answer is no, her misery abounds.

How we respond to a sky-high misery factor depends on many things. My daughter Jamie sought the quick money associated with drug trafficking, thinking all the things money could buy would bring her happiness. As I will share later, I pursued a divorce from my first husband, believing the lie that God was not enough to fill my heart and soul with deep contentment. Some people don't take such drastic and unhealthy steps but simply wallow in discontentment and self-pity. Whatever our response, the sad reality is that we often base it on an inaccurate understanding of life.

Today, at fifty-seven, I have much more realistic expectations about life and what I can or can't control. Therefore, my misery factor is generally manageable. Sure, my life still has challenges, and like anyone who is brutally honest, I still can be influenced by the world's values. For instance, I have to admit I would love to stop the aging process. But I'm reasonably satisfied simply to slow it down by maintaining a healthy lifestyle, with an occasional glycolic facial for good measure. The point is this: I live in a temporal world, and despite my heavenly security and ultimate trophy, I contend with the flesh. We all will until we reach our final destination—heaven!

So where do *you* get your expectations about life? If we believe God's Word to be true and are committed to following his precepts for a fulfilling life, we must be willing to take an honest look at our expectations. Sadly, many of us have been influenced more by television, movies, and books (even Christian ones at times) than by the Word of God.

How do you rate your misery factor? Are you deeply content most days? Are you living at peace despite the circumstances of life? Take a moment right now (if you wait, you won't do it) to list the issues in your life that produce the greatest misery. First, list the focus of your misery on the left. Then write as honestly as you can what your expectation has been in that area. Next try to accurately assess how realistic your expectations are in the light of the facts (the truth). Finally, rate your current misery factor on a scale from 1 to 10 with 10 being the most miserable you could possibly be.

Here is an example:

Issue	Expectation	Reality	Misery Rating
I am seventy-five pounds overweight.	I want to lose it all in three months.	This is unrealistic.	6
I hate my job.	I want a promotion.	My boss hates me.	10
My daughter's wedding is approaching.	I want things to be perfect.	This is impossible.	8

Now it's your turn.

Issue	Expectation	Reality	Misery Rating

Who's in Control Anyway?

My steering wheel fell off while I was driving on the freeway in 1994. It was an experience I'll never forget, and it taught me some great lessons about life and God's sovereignty. I'm here to write this—and still all in one piece to boot—so obviously the outcome was not disastrous. But it could have been. In those moments when you realize you have absolutely no control, you come to appreciate fully that every single morning you wake, and each and every breath you take, happens only because the God of the universe allows it.

In the midst of my freeway crisis, it seemed like my life, past, present, and even future, collided for a few unnerving seconds. A multitude of questions bombarded my already overstimulated mind, such as, "What have I done with my life? Does everyone I care about know how much I really love them? What will become of my children?"

I was jolted back to "real time" as my car drifted to the fast lane and then finally, while still traveling in excess of fifty miles per hour, I found myself on the shoulder of the freeway with a three-foot concrete divider quickly approaching. As my front tire made contact, I hit the brakes with all I had and came to a screeching halt after burning twenty feet of rubber along the wall. There was not a scratch on me or the car. Unbelievable.

I dropped the steering wheel in my lap and was overcome by the intensity of my heart pounding in my chest and one other startling sound. It was the rapid and loud whoosh . . . whoosh . . . whoosh of the cars on the freeway flying by me at seventy miles per hour, shaking my car violently with each pass. I realized that not one of those drivers had any idea what I had just been through. I sat there for the longest time just thinking how quickly our plans can change. I felt incredibly blessed that God had protected me from great harm. And I purposed never to forget who really has the steering wheel of my life. I must admit, all these years later, that I still on occasion grab that wheel back and act like I'm the one in charge. But God reminds me of that day, and I let go much more quickly and with less struggle than I once did.

When we experience life-changing events like steering wheels falling off, fires burning down our homes, planes flying through buildings, loved ones dying, hurricanes devastating our cities, tsunamis, and the like, we are changed profoundly. Yet, life eventually does go on no matter how great the loss. Somehow our human psyche tends to dull the experience, and we begin to live under our own steam again with our hands grasped firmly on the steering wheel of our life, driving as if we were in ultimate control.

God in his grace gives each of us incredible freedom to choose how we will live each day. In a country like America, we have the privilege of pursuing life, liberty, and even happiness. We grow up thinking this is our right. Most of us will choose our professions, spouses, and homes. We think we are in charge of our own life—and to a degree we are, if and when God allows it.

This book is about approaching life with an accurate perspective, one that acknowledges that God has the only worthwhile formula for living. He has given us his Word, which shows us clearly how to think and live with peace and joy despite our circumstances. If we truly believe the Bible is true and that God's plan for our life really is the best plan, why wouldn't we want to follow it?

In Isaiah 55:8–9, we get a glimpse of the difference between our human wisdom and God's perfect wisdom: " 'For my thoughts are not your thoughts, neither are your ways my ways,' declares the LORD. 'As the heavens are higher than the earth, so are my ways higher than your ways and my thoughts than your thoughts.' "

Pursuing the One Thing

My greatest comfort in the midst of life's never-ending challenges is the fact that God is sovereign and this life is not the ultimate prize. If we see the pleasures of today as our most important reward, we will continually make them our greatest priority. While there is nothing wrong with seeking and enjoying many of life's comforts and pleasures, they cannot be our primary objective.

The movie *City Slickers* starring Billy Crystal tells the story of three men who have become disappointed in midlife when they realize their lives are less than they had expected. So they decide to go to Montana and participate in an authentic cattle drive, hoping to rediscover their passion and purpose. When Curly, the old and weathered trail boss played by Jack Palance, and Mitch, played by Billy Crystal, are riding alone to round up some stray cattle, Curly explains that all the rest of the stuff in life "don't mean nothing" if you know the "one thing" that is the meaning of life. Mitch's interest is keenly piqued, and with great anticipation he asks Curly what that one thing is. Curly responds, "You gotta figure that out for yourself."

If Curly really knew what that "one thing" was, he would have been screaming it from every housetop (or perhaps in his case horse-top). If someone knows what can bring complete meaning to life, do you think he will actually keep that discovery to himself?

Fortunately, God does not play that kind of game with us. He desires that we learn the answers to all life's questions and gives them to us in his love letter, the Bible. The ultimate question is: What *is* the one thing that gives ultimate meaning to life? We'll explore the answer to that question at the end of chapter 2.

The Balancing Act

When you obey the call of God, the first thing that strikes you is the irrelevancy of the things you thought you had to do.

Oswald Chambers[1]

Got Time?

When I was thirty-five years old, in my most stressful season as a corporate marketing manager, the words that came out of my mouth most often were: "I am so stressed-out. I just can't take this anymore. There aren't enough hours in the day!"

How arrogant of me to think I knew more about time than God! I finally surrendered to the reality that God wasn't about to take my recommendation for a forty-eight-hour day. Although, I still have to admit that the idea of doing my hair and putting on my makeup half as many times each week would be grand.

Since the creation of the world, God has modeled the importance of rest, renewal, and balance. After six days of fashioning our universe, God rested on the seventh. Do you think he was worn out from all that work? Of course not. He's God. He simply chose to demonstrate to us what he knew we needed to thrive in a the physical world, living in perishable bodies.

God has given us a predetermined number of little twenty-four-hour packages. Each one is a precious opportunity. I don't know about you, but I want my life to count. I want to close my eyes each night and know that some part of today mattered eternally. I once heard someone say, "What I do today is important because I am paying a day of my life for it. What I accomplish must be worthwhile because the price is high." For our purposes, the word *accomplish* does not mean reaching all our worldly goals but rather investing in those things that have eternal value.

We have no idea how many days, weeks, months, or years remain for each of us. What would you do differently if you had only one year to live? What would you say to the people in your life? What would you do with your remaining time? All we have for sure is this very moment. I want to make it count for something of value.

The beloved author and Bible teacher Kay Arthur was in San Diego several months ago. I enjoyed a wonderful opportunity to spend some personal time with her and, more importantly, to hear her teach three days in a row. This seventy-five-year-old woman has more energy and passion than most women I've met who are half her age. She has the Word of God so resident in her mind that she can barely tell a personal story without Scripture flowing into her words. This experience got me thinking about how many years I have left and how I should invest them in a meaningful way. I'd love to have the passion, energy, and commitment to God's truth that Kay has when I am her age.

I'm not saying that ministry is of value because one becomes famous and reaches multitudes. That is certainly not the definition of spiritual success. Rather, any life fully committed to God and his purposes has been well invested and will be rewarded in heaven. I believe we will be amazed when we get there and realize the incredible spiritual rewards of people who prayed without ceasing and touched one life at a time. No matter where God puts us, we need to be filled with God's Word and passionate to share his truth with those he places in our lives.

I love the words of F. B. Meyer in *Meditations on the Sermon on the Mount*. He says:

> With infinite care and forethought, God has chosen the very place in which you can do your best work in the world. You may be lonely, but you have not more right to complain than the lamp has, which has been placed in a niche to illuminate a dark landing or a flight of dangerous stone steps. The Master of the house may have put you in a very small corner, on a very humble stand; but it is enough if it be His blessed will. Someday He will pass by, and you shall light His steps as He goes forth to seek and save that which is lost; or you shall kindle some great light, that shall shine like a beacon over the storm-swept ocean. Thus the obscure Andrew as the means of igniting his brother Peter, when he brought him to Jesus.[2]

One morning in my quiet time, I calculated how many days I had left if I were blessed to live to Kay's age—another nineteen years. It was 6,828 days! I found some blank pages at the end of my Bible, divided them into several columns, and wrote the number 6,828 at the top of the first column. Every day when I open my Bible, I subtract one day and write the number down. That was 160 days ago as of this writing. How fast time flies. This practice has made me more intentional (a word Kay loves to use) about each day. Of course, I have no idea how many days God has ordained for me. Psalm 39:4–5 says, "Show me, O LORD, my life's end and the number of my days; let me know how fleeting is my life. You have made my days a mere handbreadth; the span of my years is as nothing before you. Each man's life is but a breath."

We don't know how many days we have left, but we do know that God cares how we use them. If our life is totally out of balance, many days will be squandered. If we purpose to find greater balance because each day is a precious gift, lives will be touched and our sense of purpose and contentment will greatly increase—a wonderful reward for giving God our best.

Living with Margin

As we've already discovered, our misery increases when our expectations are improperly focused. One of the reasons so many of us live stressed-out, overscheduled lives is because we have unrealistic goals about what should or must be accomplished each day. We often run, run, run until a heart attack or some other kind of disaster serves as a serious wake-up call. How can we possibly add even one good thing to our day when we barely have time to get a full night's sleep? We can't unless we create a little . . . margin. To foster inner peace, we need to create margin in our lives. In his book of the same title, Dr. Richard Swenson defines margin as "the white space of life." Just imagine reading a book with one continuous run-on sentence:

NowhitespacesNomarginsNopunctuationItwouldbesofrustrating andstressproducingThatiswhatlivingwithoutmarginisallabout-NocomfortzonesYoujustwanttoscreamletmeoffthiscrazymerry goround!

Living without margin is being thirty minutes late to your doctor's appointment, because you were late getting the kids to school, because you ran out of gas two blocks from the gas station, because you were late getting home last night and decided to wait until morning to fill up . . . but you overslept because you were overtired.

Life is like a rubber band. If we are stretched too often or too far, we eventually snap! As Dr. Swenson writes:

Living without margin is not having time to finish the book you're reading on stress. Margin is having time to read it twice. Living without margin is fatigue. Margin is energy. Living without margin is red ink. Margin is black ink. Living without margin is hurry. Margin is calm. Living without margin is anxiety. Margin is security.[3]

Do you wonder why I have dedicated an entire chapter to the subject of balance? Because so few people can maintain it for long periods of time. By simple definition, balance means "a state of equilibrium." In my opinion, true life balance is equilibrium of body, soul, and spirit. If our spiritual life is in balance, it will dramatically affect the balance of our body and soul. Many of us need to implement some simple principles to help us live more purposefully in our daily lives so we can relax emotionally and focus on our relationship with God.

Here are a few practical tips that may help you restore some margin in your life:

1. Expect the unexpected.
2. When scheduling your plans, increase your time window to decrease rushing.
3. Learn to say no to the good, so you can say yes to the best!
4. Prune your activities to essentials whenever you can.
5. Cut your to-do list for today in half and expect it to take twice the time you think.
6. Release yourself from the hyper-speed mentality of the world and release others also.
7. Get less done . . . but do the right things!
8. Create your own buffer zones—schedule free time for both daily and weekly renewal.

True Balance

Living a life of balance does not mean that we become ultraefficient time-management experts. It does mean that we adjust moment to moment to life's surprises and God's divine appointments. By simplifying our calendars wherever we can and adjusting our expectations, we can respond to life more intentionally. The balanced life is not an easy, stress-free life. But it is a life that keeps bouncing back like one of those weighted children's toys that won't stay down when you push it over.

Jesus said in Matthew 16:26: "What good will it be for a man if he gains the whole world, yet forfeits his soul?" We stress about and strive after many things yet often miss the "one thing" entirely. Our life is a constant balancing act between living in this temporal world and keeping our hearts and minds on heaven.

The lack of control and unrealistic expectations we discussed in the last chapter can cause us to respond in out-of-balance ways that increase our stress and throw our lives into chaos. So by now (if you are anything like me), you may feel both convicted and guilty. That's not always such a bad thing, if it helps you take appropriate action. But wait! Before you set a goal or make a promise to God, give yourself a little grace. You didn't get this way overnight, and you probably won't change overnight either. Take one day at a time and make one or two small changes. As I discuss in detail in my book *Change Your Habits, Change Your Life*, it takes at least twenty-one days to even *begin* to change old, unhealthy habits. We need to let go of old black-or-white, all-or-nothing attitudes and do the best we can each day to move in a more positive direction. That is why this book includes a forty-day journey. Each day, you can invest in changing your thoughts, attitudes, and actions in God-honoring ways so at the end of your life he will say, "Well done, good and faithful servant! You have been faithful with a few things; I will put you in charge of many things. Come and share your master's happiness!" (Matt. 25:23).

We live in mortal bodies that are confined to time and space. We have souls that are piloted by our minds and driven by a free will that often rebels against our Creator. We are also spiritual beings who are connected to God through Christ if we believe in him and that his shed blood is the only way we can be saved. Since we exist in those three dimensions, it makes sense to explore all three and some important biblical perspectives that can keep us focused on God's best plan for our lives. Perhaps an illustration I have shared many times will give you a good visual example.

Juggling the Balls of Life

It's been said that life is like juggling a variety of balls—always trying to keep them all in the air without dropping any. In my estimation, some of those balls (or life areas) are more fragile than others. Our work, daily chores, and to-do lists are much like rubber balls. No matter how many times we drop them, they just keep bouncing back. The phone rings, email pops up, bills arrive, and to-do lists grow—day after day, week after week. When you wash clothes or dishes, dirty ones reappear within hours. The tyranny of the urgent drowns out the truly essential much too often. We wake up every day and do the same things all over again. Then we wonder if this is all there is to our life. What would happen if you minimized the time you invested and the importance you placed on these rubber balls of life so you could invest in the more fragile glass balls of life?

The glass balls of life include our physical and mental life areas as well as our relationships with others. Our emotions are responders to our beliefs and are in essence a part of our mental process, all of which encompasses our soul. These fragile balls become nicked, cracked, and sometimes even shattered if we neglect or drop them too often. In the physical dimension, we often see our bodies as rubber balls in our youth because they seem to bounce back. But those of us who are over forty know this is not true. In the mental dimension, unhealthy thinking and attitudes can create "cracks" in the glass ball of our mind and influence our attitude, emotions, and behavior in unhealthy ways. I will discuss the habits of our mind and how crucial they are to dynamic, lasting change in chapter 3.

Our personal relationships are also glass balls. Neglect may result in broken friendships, rebellious children, or destroyed marriages. These glass balls of life need consistent care and attention even though they are not as demanding as the rubber balls of life.

Our spiritual life can be compared to a different kind of ball—a balloon. A completely deflated balloon represents the spiritual vacuum that exists before we have a personal relationship with Christ. This deflated balloon has no power and takes up very little space in our lives. But when we receive Christ as our personal Savior, the Holy Spirit comes to take up residence in our spirit and we become "inflated." At first we are filled with the Spirit, but we lack power because we don't have the Word of God "richly dwelling in us." As we nourish our minds and spirits with his truth, pray, and worship, our spiritual balloon grows and grows. It expands fully and begins to influence our thoughts and behavior more and more.

A full spiritual balloon ensures that our perspectives about life are accurate. As we fill our mind with God's Word, the Holy Spirit is able to activate his power in our life. As we pray and become intimate with God, we begin to appreciate with fresh insight our true identity in Christ. As we seek to live within his will and choose to surrender to his power and plan, we find that many of our goals and aspirations lose their appeal. Without daily filling, our spiritual lives can fizzle out, just like a blown-up balloon that is released into the air without its end tied. We don't lose Christ or the Holy Spirit, but we do lose the power to walk with victory.

How do we effectively juggle the balls of life? How do we create enough margin in our lives to allow more time for the glass balls and the spiritual balloon? We must *choose* moment to moment. Because I made so many bad choices in decades past, a quote by Edwin Louis Cole continues to resonate in my soul and remind me frequently why our small, daily choices are so important. He said, "Everything is under the power of choice, but once that choice has been made, we become a servant to it."[4]

Choosing the best over and over will eventually result in a more balanced and rewarding life. That does not mean you will become the poster child of efficiency. Your life may remain disorganized. A multitude of rubber balls may continually bounce in your direction. The difference will be more internal than anything else. Choose to focus and give more time to the truly important things in your life by asking yourself questions such as:

- Will it help me know and love God more?
- Will it help me know and love my spouse more?
- Will it help me know and love my children more?
- Will it help me grow in loving others more?

Living in balance was an issue long before our hyper-speed new millennium. Even in the time of Christ, some struggled to choose the best from all the good. God has graciously given us many examples of people who lived with the wrong focus. We are not alone in our struggle, yet God does not want us to stay stuck. For many, the story of two very different sisters resonates in our hearts and reminds us to choose "the good part." Which sister do you most resemble?

The Original Martha

When the name Martha is used today, we often think about the famous Martha Stewart who is known for her incredible ability to cook, decorate, and design fabulous things with apparent ease. She is the ultimate domestic superwoman in many people's eyes. This modern-day Martha was not the first Martha to be concerned about household excellence. In Luke 10:38–42, we read about a special encounter Jesus had with two sisters.

Now as they were traveling along, He entered a village; and a woman named Martha welcomed Him into her home. She had a sister called

Mary, who was seated at the Lord's feet, listening to His word. But Martha was distracted with all her preparations; and she came up to Him and said, "Lord, do You not care that my sister has left me to do all the serving alone? Then tell her to help me." But the Lord answered and said to her, "Martha, Martha, you are worried and bothered about so many things; but only one thing is necessary, for Mary has chosen the good part, which shall not be taken away from her." (NASB)

Martha is so confident that she is right and her sister is wrong, that when she asks Jesus the question, "Do You not care that my sister has left me to do all the serving alone?" she doesn't even give him a moment to respond. Instead, she assumes he sees her point and actually tells the King of Kings what to say. Wow. To be quite honest, I think I've done that on occasion in my prayers. I may ask God, "Please show my friend how selfish she is, or my husband how neglectful he has been," and so on. But of course God sees and knows the entire picture. Perhaps I am the one who is being selfish or insensitive to the other person's needs. When we ask God for an answer, we must be careful to listen for it.

Jesus responds to Martha much differently than she expected. He says, "Martha, Martha" instead of simply "Martha." I'm sure he needed to say her name twice to get her attention, since she wasn't really listening in the first place. Then he tells her exactly what she doesn't want to hear but what she needs to know: "You are worried and bothered about so many things." That is the last thing I want to hear from my husband when I'm preparing for a dinner party. I think my recipes and table setting are pretty important. But if I'm getting the whole household stressed-out and neglecting my guests, the party really isn't a success at all.

Now just imagine hearing those words from the mouth of the Lord directed to *you*. Sometimes the truth hurts. One thing I know for sure is that Jesus loved Martha just as much as he loved Mary. His intention was not to hurt or tear Martha down. His motive was to turn her toward what really mattered. And that's exactly what his next words describe when he says, "But only one thing is necessary, for Mary has chosen the good part, which shall not be taken away from her."

The first few times I read this passage, I felt sorry for Martha. How embarrassing and belittling to be compared to the sister who was sitting there doing *nothing*. But after studying the passage more and thinking about how much Jesus loves us all despite our weaknesses, I realized that he did not rebuke Martha to shame her but rather to ensure that she did not continue to miss the "one thing." If we don't slow down and sit at Jesus's feet, we will never experience life as he intended. The one thing we must focus on—the meaning of life itself—is distilled in the following words of Christ:

> Jesus replied: " 'Love the Lord your God with all your heart and with all your soul and with all your mind.' This is the first and greatest commandment. And the second is like it: 'Love your neighbor as yourself.' All the Law and the Prophets hang on these two commandments."
>
> Matthew 22:37–40

Loving God fully is our purpose. It is a lifelong quest, and we never fully arrive. But as we surrender to his will, trust fully in his Word, and follow him with all our hearts, we slowly fall in love with him more and more. If our busyness and plans are getting us so stressed-out and distracted that we aren't spending quality time with God, then we will never love him with our entire being. If loving God is our "one thing," then we must invest our thoughts and energy on making that our most important lifelong quest.

We don't know how Martha responded to Jesus's words. We don't have any more information about this encounter than what is written above. But I'm guessing that if Martha had responded immediately and sat down with Mary, we probably would have read about it. Only God knows for sure. Too often our egos get in the way and we become resistive to life-changing advice. We think our way is the best way and in self-defense close off our minds and hearts. It is that kind of thinking that got Martha (and many of us) into trouble in the first place.

Psalm 46:10 says, "Be still, and know that I am God." It is so hard to sit down and be still. There is so much to be done. So we run along at hyper-speed and too often miss the most important "one thing." It's interesting to note that the New American Standard Bible translates this same verse: "*Cease striving* and know that I am God." The Hebrew word for "be still" or "cease striving" is *raphah*, which means to cease, be feeble, be idle, let alone, be still or weak.

We need to slow down, be quiet, and realize our complete weakness without God. By acknowledging our feebleness and inadequacy, we can see his immensity, perfection, and sovereignty more clearly. It is in this realization that we begin to comprehend the futility of our striving and busyness. It is in this comprehension of the eternal perspective that we can let go of the anxiety and frustrations of daily living and find peace and joy in the midst of life's storms.

There were times in the last ten years when I stopped looking for Scripture verses to validate my needs and sought instead simply to study God's Word and let it speak to me without my own agenda being part of my motivation. In that time of surrendered study, God began a new work in me. Sometimes it felt like a rug was being pulled out from under me. But in the long run, I realized that truth is truth and I needed to learn to pursue and accept it with passion.

Think about this: None of us would say, "I don't believe there is really electricity coming out of the electrical socket, so I'm just going to stick the point of this knife in there to prove it." We would be foolish to do so because we'd get shocked in the process! Just because we can't see something or don't understand it does not mean it doesn't exist or have power. God's power is not always perceived and is never fully understood, but it is powerful just the same. The Word of God is sharper than any two-edged sword. It divides lies and truth (Heb. 4:12). If we submit our entire life to its scrutiny, we'll never get "shocked."

I've come to understand a basic principle. It is simply this: When we seek God first, set our minds on his Word, and choose his ways over ours, life works pretty well even in the most difficult of times. It is my prayer that this book will help you establish a godly expectation about your life that is in sync with the reality of God's Word. In turn, he will turn your mourning into gladness and will give you comfort and joy instead of sorrow (Jer. 31:13).

Life's Defining Habits

What you think and do every day defines you. So who are you? And what happened to your life?

Every weekday morning, you will find my friend and pastor, Tim Scott, at a local Starbucks with his laptop open, studying the Word of God and preparing his Sunday message. He has practiced this habit for more than thirty years. Well, it wasn't always Starbucks and a laptop—but it was always a coffee shop and the Word of God.

Our habits ultimately define our lives. We are all creatures of habit. The important question is, "Are my habits positive or negative?" It is essential that we explore our habits and how significantly they impact our lives as a part of our journey toward greater passion, contentment, and joy.

The subjects of habits and change have been key themes in my writing and speaking for more than fifteen years. Really bad habits led me to the Lord. My misery gave me a powerful reason to change. Christ's blood and the living Word gave me the means to do it. Christ has renewed my mind, transformed my thinking, and regenerated my life. I am forever grateful that I was blessed to personally experience how his truth really can set us free. That is why I write and speak. I know the pain of being in bondage to unhealthy thinking and habits. I'm not just talking about the usual lifestyle habits. I'm talking about *all* your habits: How you think. How you live. What you think and do every day defines you. So who are you? And what happened to your life?

If you want some in-depth teaching on the dynamics of change, I encourage you to read my last book, *Change Your Habits, Change Your Life*. For our purposes here, I will address some key principles that can dramatically affect your ability to implement the teaching of this book and move you toward a life fully surrendered to God.

How You Think

In his book *Habits of the Mind*, Christian psychologist Dr. Archibald Hart writes:

> The modern mind is corrupt, not only because it is sinful, but because it is dominated by unhealthy habits. Let me put the issue to you in a nutshell: Who you are, as a Christian believer, can be no better and no worse than the thoughts you entertain in your head. Who you are emotionally can never transcend your level of thinking. Your thought process is a ceiling beyond which you cannot aspire. Your brain is no stronger than your weakest thought, and your character is no more virtuous than your most private reflections.[1]

As I have said many times, and the Bible clearly confirms, we are what we think. The quality of our thought life is an incredibly important influence on the quality of our life. That is why God's Word addresses this topic extensively. Dr. Hart continues in the introduction to his book:

> Your thinking determines whether you move toward disease or health, success or failure, achievement or decline. It influences whether you

will live a long or short life and whether you will be happy or sad most of the time. It even determines if you'll get married and whether your sex life will be satisfying.[2]

If our thinking is that powerful, then it makes perfect sense to put biblical, healthy thinking at the top of our to-do list every day. Dr. Hart teaches that healthy thinking is a habit that must be learned. I know from both personal experience and as a Christian life coach that this is exactly right. In addition, all feelings and actions are an outflow of our thoughts. Therefore, it is essential to know what you think, identify the lies, and replace them with truth. In our forty-day journey, we will take time to do that—relative to the devotion for each day. Before we begin that journey, it makes sense to identify some of the major lies we believe and begin the process of replacing them.

In Romans 12:2, Paul writes, "Do not conform any longer to the pattern of this world, but be transformed by the renewing of your mind." We live in a world that bombards us with messages—mostly negative—all day long. We are influenced by everything we see and hear, and we measure ourselves in comparison to others. If our influence is mostly worldly, our perspectives will be the same. On the other hand, if it is mostly godly—focused on truth from God's Word—our perspectives will be healthy and accurate. It is clear from this verse that Paul is telling us to stop following the world's way of thinking and acting and renew our minds in a way that will transform our lives. Truth transforms. Complete, God-honoring truth comes only from the Bible.

If you are chronically discontent, joyless, frustrated, or consistently experience any other negative emotion, it is because you are chronically thinking discontented, joyless, and frustrated thoughts. I know that sounds simplistic, but it is true. In Philippians 4:8, we are given a beautiful prescription for healthy thinking. Paul says, "Finally, brothers, whatever is true, whatever is noble, whatever is right, whatever is pure, whatever is lovely, whatever is admirable—if anything is excellent or praiseworthy—think about such things." We must intentionally focus on that which is worth our attention. If we fill our mind with excellent and praiseworthy things (God and his Word), we will be transformed by the renewing of our mind.

There are four steps we must take to effectively renew our minds. I taught these principles in *Change Your Habits, Change Your Life* and will briefly review them here. They include:

1. Set your mind
2. Identify the lies you believe
3. Replace the lies with truth
4. Practice healthy self-talk

Step #1: Set Your Mind

Numerous Scripture passages teach the importance of choosing what we think about, sometimes using the phrase "set your mind." When we set a clock, we purposely change the hour and minute to reflect something new. We can set our mind in the same way by purposely changing our focus. Colossians 3:1–2 says, "Since, then, you have been raised with Christ, *set your hearts* on things above, where Christ is seated at the right hand of God. *Set your minds* on things above, not on earthly things" (emphasis added).

In Ephesians 4:22–24, we are told, "You were taught, with regard to your former way of life, to *put off your old self*, which is being corrupted by its deceitful desires; to be made new in the *attitude of your minds*; and to *put on* the new self, created to be like God in true righteousness and holiness" (emphasis added).

It is clear we are instructed to take personal responsibility and action when it comes to our thinking by setting our hearts and minds, putting off our old self, and putting on our new self. All those actions will ultimately make us "new in the attitudes of our minds." If we don't do these things, we become willing victims of our own unhealthy mind-set.

In Romans 8:5, we learn that we must choose where we will set our mind. "Those who live according to the sinful nature have their *minds set* on what that nature desires; but those who live in accordance with the Spirit have their *minds set* on what the Spirit desires" (emphasis added). Believers have power over sin, yet they don't always exercise it. They can choose to set their minds on natural desires. We often use the excuse of our feelings, as if they had minds of their own rather than being a response to our most frequent thoughts. We have a choice. And if we want a life that brings deep satisfaction and honors God, we must set our minds on what the Spirit desires. We will talk more about that and walking by the Spirit in chapter 5.

We believe what we tell ourselves most often, and therefore our most dominant thoughts drive our feelings and our actions. If we want to change either, we must make a conscious decision to continually "reset" our thinking throughout the day. When you catch yourself thinking or saying things that are not "excellent or praiseworthy," stop and set your mind on that which *is* worth thinking about.

Step #2: Identify the Lies You Believe

Sometimes we are not fully aware of the unhealthy thinking and resulting lies that have come to drive our feelings and behavior. We have believed them for so long that we don't even know they are creating automatic responses and killing our joy. If you are not sure what lies you believe, one way to begin to expose them is to follow the trail of negative emotions and actions. For example, if you are frequently angry, ask yourself, "What am I angry about?" Perhaps you feel like people don't respect you or that you have been treated unfairly your entire life. If you frequently lash out verbally or spend hours each day being lazy, ask yourself why you are acting this way. Write down all the negative emotions and actions that may be affecting the quality of your life. Take a minute or two, *right now*, and ask God to give you insight. Write down what immediately comes to mind. Then try to identify the lies that may be associated with them.

My negative emotions or behavior are:

The lies I may believe are:

Don't worry if you have a hard time with this exercise. Just try to become more aware of your unhealthy thinking and practice setting your mind on things above every time you begin to think, act, or feel in an unhealthy way. It's not essential that you immediately identify every lie. However, it is essential to fill your mind with life-changing truth. That is easy to identify. Just open your Bible.

Step #3: Replace the Lies with Truth

During our forty-day journey, you will have the opportunity each day to ask yourself if there are any lies you believe related to the devotional teaching for that day and to identify the truth from within the teaching that can replace that lie. I encourage you to do this all the time. Try to become hypersensitive to your thought life and stop yourself from feeding your mind those negative messages any longer. As you purpose to do this, you will become more aware of your thoughts and hopefully will take positive action to change them.

After several years of taking amphetamines to bring my out-of-control bulimia under control (or so I thought), I began to have panic attacks. They lasted for five years and became debilitating over time. I actually thought I was losing my mind or dying—perhaps both. My fear led me to God. I learned about the power of renewing my mind very early in my Christian walk. I believed many lies. I believed that I was losing my mind and was unable to control my feelings or behavior.

God in his grace allowed me to find a life-changing Scripture passage. Second Timothy 1:7 says, "For God has not given us a spirit of fear, but of power and of love and of a sound mind" (NKJV). Those words were like water in the desert to my parched soul. I said that verse twenty or thirty times a day for many months. Without fully understanding the biblical concept of "setting my mind," that is exactly what I did. I forced myself to stop focusing on my fears and to set my mind on God's truth. I reminded myself that I had never died before, and if I did, at least now I knew where I was going! I told myself that God was always with me and that I need not live in fear. Within about a month, my panic attacks occurred less frequently, and when they did come, they were less severe. By the end of the year, they were gone completely. No therapy, no drugs—just life-changing truth renewing my mind and transforming me.

Two things happened to me. First, the neuron pathways in my mind began to physically change. The old message pathways began to shrink because I was no longer "feeding" them, and the new messages began to grow, eventually becoming like superhighways in my mind. While my description is simplistic, this is medically accurate and verifiable. God designed the brain to respond in this way . . . whether you believe in him or not. With the exception of mental illness and brain pathology (including chemical depression), we can significantly transform our brain's "wiring" by erasing and replacing old, unhealthy thought patterns with new, life-changing truth. We are all "brainwashed" by our thoughts. Do you want to be brainwashed with truth or lies?

The second thing that happened was totally supernatural. Hebrews 4:12 says, "For the word of God is living and active. Sharper than any double-edged sword, it penetrates even to dividing soul and spirit, joints and marrow; it judges the thoughts and attitudes of the heart." God's Word is living and active. I have experienced this many times in my life. The double-edged sword in this case is more like a surgical knife that we turn on ourselves. It is able to cut out the lies we believe (judging the thoughts and attitudes of the heart) and replace them with penetrating truth. For truth to lock in permanently, however, we must be sure to practice step #4.

Step #4: Practice Healthy Self-Talk

Knowing truth is not enough to change us—we must *believe* it. Truth needs to move from knowledge to faith and from our head to our heart. This happens only after significant repetition. Remember what I said before: We believe what we tell ourselves most often.

For our neuron pathways to change and the living Word to cut out the lies and replace them with truth, we must expose our minds repeatedly to that truth. It would be very dangerous if God designed our brains in such a way that our thinking and behavior changed by being exposed to a thought once or twice. We would all be like a bunch of robots turning right and left as if we were reprogrammed with every new thought or idea.

Thankfully, that is not the case. God calls us to be good stewards of our minds, taking purposeful action to guard them from lies and to infuse them with truth. We don't fill up our mind once, seal it, and move on. If you want to effectively erase and replace your lies, you need to tell yourself the truth every day for months. On a purely physical level, your neuron pathways will begin to change in small ways in about twenty-one days. Of course, God in his supernatural power can do whatever he wants in whatever time frame he chooses.

If you want to renew your mind in one or more key areas, I encourage you to ask the Lord to draw you to a Scripture passage that is relevant to your current life challenges. Use it as I did 2 Timothy 1:7. Memorize it and repeat it to yourself each and every time your thoughts start to revert to the lie you believe. Do this for as long as it takes—perhaps many months—and watch the power of the living Word renew your mind and life!

We also need healthy role models to demonstrate healthy thinking and behavior. A fitting model can be found in the apostle Paul.

After he tells us *what* to think about (as we read earlier) in Philippians 4:8, he makes a statement in verse 9 that is so outrageous that you could consider him arrogant—but don't judge him too harshly. He earned the right to say these words by the life he had led since the day he had met the risen Christ on the road to Damascus. This is what he wrote: "Whatever you have learned or received or heard from me, or seen in me—put it into practice. And the God of peace will be with you."

Can you say that to anyone? Imagine telling your friends, "Whatever you learn from me, hear or see me do . . . do it! And if you do, God's peace will be with you." I'd like to be able to say that. I have some areas in my life that I could recommend others follow—but *whatever* I say or do? I'm sure not there yet. The point is that we need excellent role models and teachers. No one person in your life will be a great model in every area. But many different godly people may provide good teaching or modeling that you can use. We all want God's peace. With it comes a sense of calm and contentment. Paul is essentially saying, "Think about the right things (v. 8), learn from the right people, and repeatedly practice their good example (v. 9)."

The word *practice* means that something must be done over and over in order for it to be effective. The old cliché "practice makes perfect" is actually inaccurate. The truth is "practice makes permanent." For years, I have used healthy self-talk tapes and CDs related to my teaching to help my readers and clients renew their minds with God-honoring messages. I wrote and produced a CD specific to both *Scale Down* and *Change Your Habits*. I will also create one specific to this book. There is more information about that in the resource section at the back of the book. You also can make your own CDs or simply write messages on index cards or Post-it notes and read them until they become part of your habitual thinking. Whatever you do, do it repeatedly.

Paul's excellent role model prompted me to ask several godly women I know to share their personal stories as a means of encouragement to you. Some of you have been betrayed . . . so was Kimberly. Others have never been married or experienced the thrill of motherhood . . . neither has Diana or Sylvia. Some of you have created your own messes . . . I can meet you there. In chapter 6, these women speak to a variety of life circumstances that could leave one feeling joyless and discontent. Yet, they all turned their eyes upward and found strength and hope in the midst of their trials. Today they are wonderful examples of women who live consistently joyful and contented lives. Now don't skip ahead. We have some important ground to cover before we get to their stories.

How You Live

Hopefully you have come to appreciate the fact that your habits flow out of your most dominant thoughts and attitudes. While lasting change must start in the mind, it is still very important to honestly assess your habits. From the time you get up in the morning until you go to bed at night, you make decisions about investing your time. You may think that many choices are out of your control, especially if you spend many hours at a job or have a big family to manage. But even the choice of how you start the first few minutes of your day and what you do during your lunch break matter. How you invest those moments can literally change your life.

Exploring the importance of your daily habits could easily be a book topic in itself. But for the purposes of *this* book, I simply want to ask you a few questions, have you reflect on the answers, and ask God to direct you in how to respond. My central objective is to encourage you to become more aware of your daily habits and the positive changes you can make to transform your life.

The following list contains a variety of common daily activities. For each, I provide a few possible options as examples (some better than others) and an "other" option where you can write your own answer (unless one of mine actually fits). Circle an option that fits or fill in your own answer for each category below:

The first thing I do each morning when I wake up is:
1. Set my mind on things above and thank God for the day
2. Hit the snooze button and wish I could sleep more
3. Other: _____

Once I am up and fully awake, I:
1. Spend time in the Word and prayer
2. Eat breakfast and get ready for the day
3. Other: _____

My number one priority most days is:
1. Becoming more intimate with God
2. Surviving
3. Other: _____

When I have a few free moments during the day, I
1. Read or listen to something that "sets my mind on things above"
2. Go shopping
3. Other: _____

My physical habits include:
1. Eating a reasonable amount of nutritious food and getting exercise most days
2. Eating too much and moving too little
3. Other: _____

In the evening, I look forward to:
1. Spending some quiet time reflecting on my day and relaxing with family or friends

2. Watching television or going out and having fun

3. Other: _____

In my material life, my priority is:

    1. God and his purposes

    2. My bills and personal needs

    3. Other: _____

When I have a conflict with someone, I usually:

    1. Seek God's wisdom before I speak and measure my words carefully

    2. Say what's on my mind first and think later

    3. Other: _____

When I am tempted to sin, my habit is to:

    1. Flee from temptation and draw near to God

    2. Cave in and ask for forgiveness later

    3. Other: _____

This list is obviously limited, but I hope it allowed you to gain some insight into your daily habits and identify areas that are in serious need of change. As I wrote the list, I certainly became convicted of my own areas of weakness. This exercise is not intended to make you feel guilty but rather to help you realize that we all choose how we will respond to every aspect of life. For those who circled many number one choices, good for you. But never forget that God cares more about our inward motives than our outward actions. In other words, godly habits done out of a legalistic mind-set do not glorify God. He wants our love for him to drive our behavior. That is why we cannot just evaluate our actions; we must evaluate our thoughts and beliefs. Good action without a changed heart means nothing to God.

Before we close this chapter, I would like you to participate in one more exercise designed to help you identify the things about your life that you find most challenging or disappointing. Simply read the phrase and write whatever comes to mind in the blank space provided.

1. My life would be so much better if _____

_____

2. The habit I need to change so I can move forward is_____

_____

3. The sin I need to confess and turn away from is _____

_____

Take some time to think and pray about your answers to these questions. Are any lies peeking out from your words? Do you believe God cares about you and wants you to experience the abundant life that Christ speaks about? I can assure you that he does and that the process you are beginning within the pages of this book is an important step toward rediscovering the joy of Christ in your daily life.

4

The Cancer of Discontentment

You say, "If I had a little more, I should be very satisfied." You make a mistake. If you are not content with what you have, you will not be satisfied if it were doubled.

Charles Spurgeon[1]

"I don't mean to insult you," she began, "but the reason you feel so awful about everything is because your focus is totally about you!" Well, *that* hurt! And of course it was about me! I was the one with the shallow husband, not *her*. She was my Christian friend, and I felt she was being judgmental and unfair. The Bible says we are not to judge each other, doesn't it? Well, she was judging me, and I assumed all my other Christian friends would too, so I ran as far as I could from church and anything remotely religious. My life was not what I'd signed up for, and I was confused and unhappy. My marriage was not turning out as I had planned, and I was ticked off. I didn't want to be one of those women plodding through each day without passion, contentment, and joy. But that is exactly what I was doing.

True Confessions

I want to share a part of my story that I have never written about specifically. If you've read any of my other books, you know that I am quite transparent about many of my past failings. I've shared my tale of dieting, bulimia, amphetamine use, and panic attacks in-depth in other books. Those trials brought me to the Lord. In my weakness, he revealed the path to victory. I followed God's lead and wisdom closely for the first seven years of my walk with him. But somewhere in the eighth year, I stopped believing he could fulfill *all* my needs in every area of my life.

In the past two years, God has been nudging me to share the entire story of my failed marriage, which ended in 1984, because it is a prime illustration of what can happen when we let discontentment and self-fulfillment get out of control. Our unhappiness affects not only our lives but also the lives of others . . . dramatically. In my case, it almost destroyed my daughters. In the story that follows, I have changed the names of my former husband and step-son to protect their privacy. I am sharing my story from my perspective at the time and by no means am blaming anyone other than myself. This story is about my mistakes and no one else's. I am simply sharing a few of the details so you can see how insidious discontentment can become.

Unfortunately, my story is not unique. Christian marriages around the nation are disintegrating at alarming rates.[2] Perhaps your issue has nothing to do with marriage and divorce. However, many of us have a season when our own self-centered approach to life hurts the people around us as well as ourselves. The circumstance may be different for you, but the ultimate truths will still apply. My desire is that you will discover insight and hope that will move you through those seasons in a way that honors God and uplifts others.

If you are discontent in your marriage, it is my prayer that you will reconsider your role in ending "what God has joined together"

(Mark 10:9). I cannot undo the past, but perhaps some of you can do your part to salvage your marriages, protect the hearts of your children, and honor God by trusting him for your future. For those who cannot stop the freight train of divorce threatening to mow down your life, follow the lead of Kimberly (you'll read her story in chapter 6) and hang on to God with all your might. He will get you through!

My Story

By the time I was nineteen, I was like an out-of-control alcoholic—except my addiction was to food. The only reason I was not obese was because I binged and purged, sometimes four or five times a day. At the time, I was about thirty pounds overweight by healthy standards. Fortunately, at 5 feet, 7 inches tall, I hid my excess weight fairly well. During that time, I rotated my out-of-control eating and bulimia with periods of total fasting by using diet pills. They completely eliminated my desire to eat—something I absolutely relished. However, if I took them too often, I became very anxious, and my increasing panic attacks took over like a force outside myself. During this season, I broke up with my high school sweetheart of five years and found myself very alone. I felt fat, ugly, and pathetic. I was in my first year of nursing school and just barely making it to class each day after a hefty dose of Valium, which tranquilized my fear long enough for me to get through lectures and clinical time at the hospital. Amazingly, no one knew I was falling apart at the seams.

In this self-destructive time, I met John. He was nine years older than me, athletic, attractive, and a high school PE teacher and coach. He was the opposite of my old boyfriend, who was reckless and ir-responsible. John took me on dates and actually paid for everything. He had a beautiful apartment in downtown Seattle with a gorgeous view. In my eyes, he was mature, stable, and perfect.

John had been married before, but his wife had left him for another man. They had a darling little boy, Jason, who was four when I met him. John was a terrific father and concerned about his son's well-being. Several months after we began dating, he took full custody of Jason. We had great times together, and John loved that I would babysit whenever he asked so he could play golf. I knew deep down that he was judging my mothering skills, so I wowed him with my attentiveness to his son. I wasn't thrilled about being a mom in my early twenties, but if Jason came with the "John package," I could not have asked for a better kid. It wasn't a bad deal if I got Mr. Perfect in the long run. Over time, I fell in love. At least that's what I thought. I realized many years later that I was in love with the idea of being in love.

There was, however, one little problem with Mr. Perfect—he wanted me to be thinner. At first, John told me how beautiful I was. But over time, he made it clear that my generous thighs and backside were more than he could fully appreciate. (If he'd only known that the days of J Lo were coming!) The pressure for me to get thin was pretty intense. To his credit, John had no idea of the struggles I faced with food and bulimia. (In fact, he would never know.) I tried my best to lose weight, but instead my bulimia became more out of control than ever. I went back on the diet pills and lost thirty pounds, and soon the scale read 120. John asked me to marry him on my twenty-first birthday.

A Rocky Start

I stood at the end of the church aisle holding my father's arm, and as the wedding march began, I felt my heart beating in my throat. I asked Dad to wait because I wasn't ready to walk down the aisle. Deep in my heart I knew I was making a mistake. He thought it was bridal jitters and said, "It's time, honey, let's go," and the next thing I knew I was saying, "I do." But inside I was screaming, "I don't. I don't!"

I packed my scale in my suitcase for the honeymoon out of fear that I'd gain weight if I did not consult it every day and prayed that I had not made a huge mistake in marrying John. The fact that we started our honeymoon golfing in Victoria, British Columbia (an activity I hate to this day), and then finished by taking his son to Disneyland was a pretty good clue that I was not living out my dream.

None of this was poor John's fault. I mean, what man *wouldn't* want to golf and go to Disneyland on his honeymoon if you let him? I simply was too young and immature to stand up for myself and make the right choices. I was so enraptured with the idea of marriage and having a stable man in my life that I jumped at the first possibility. I also had no spiritual direction, nor did John. We were relying on our feelings (more accurately hormones) to lead us.

Our marriage got off to a rocky start. I did not feel in love with John, and when I noticed other men who seemed better suited to me, I felt angry and stuck. In my skewed assessment, he seemed to care only about my role as a mom and a trophy—but not about me.

Despite the fact that I had flushed all my diet pills down the toilet and had vowed never to take them again, my panic attacks became more severe. When I ran to John for comfort and support, he shut down. His former wife had experienced episodes of bizarre behavior before she divorced him, and he feared I was on the same path. I had never felt so alone in all my life.

The next two years were a blur for me. I made it through nursing school with terrific grades despite the panic attacks, but I was exhausted all the time and felt emotionally bankrupt. I needed someone to comfort and understand me. Soon the anxiety followed me all day long. I went to medical doctors, who in turn sent me to psychologists and psychiatrists. No one had any answers, and the darkness was closing in. Many days, I truly believed I was losing my mind. I began to have such severe episodes that I actually felt like I was dying. The fear perpetuated fear, and I felt consumed by darkness.

One night, I feared for my life and called out to God in desperation to help me. I had no idea how to find him, but I knew he was the only one who could save me. In his grace, he brought to mind the only woman I knew who could be considered "religious." In the midst of a panic attack, I called her on the phone and blurted out, "Tonette, do you know God?" She assured me she did and, more importantly, that he knew *me*. Tonette shared the gospel with me, and I asked Christ into my life that night. Soon after, my husband and I began going to church together, and he also accepted Christ. My entire life changed dramatically in a few short weeks.

Transformed by the Renewing of My Mind

It was my heart's desire for God to take away my panic attacks and eating issues immediately. As I shared in the previous chapter, he did just that . . . over time. Within six months, I knew that he was transforming me, and by the end of the year, I was amazed that the woman who once lived in constant fear and anxiety was now celebrating life with great joy. I was so excited about my new relationship with Jesus that I wanted absolutely everyone to know about him. At the time, I was a brand-new registered nurse at a large hospital in downtown Seattle. I worked on a medical floor that dealt with many diseases, not the least of which was cancer. Every day, I treated patients who were facing death, and I felt personally responsible for their souls. Fortunately, I had a wonderful pastor who helped me understand that my job was to plant seeds and God's job was to save souls. I share all this to validate that my walk with God was authentic. I trusted in Christ alone for my salvation, I was a new creation, and my faith was strong. Years later, it would be easy to doubt such statements by my actions.

Since becoming a Christian, I have come to understand that even though we are saved by grace, we can still follow our own path of sin and destruction. We are saved in an instant when we believe that we are sinners separated from God and that our only hope is the blood of Christ poured out for the sins of the world. Yet, we are sanctified (separated and made perfect) over a lifetime but never completely until heaven. Some of us will make more progress than others in this life.

The next few years were full and blessed. Near our fourth anniversary, I found out I was pregnant, and I gave birth to our first daughter, Jamie, on February 9, 1977. I wanted to be the perfect mom above all else and relished every moment with my beautiful little girl. John was concerned about our finances, so I went back to work part-time in the labor and delivery unit and absolutely loved my work. Soon our second daughter, Jill, was conceived, and the little firecracker was born on July 4, 1980. I remember being in the hospital shortly after the delivery, holding Jill in my arms and praying. The thought came to my mind, "My life is perfect. This is the best it will ever get." And then, for some crazy reason—be it hormones or the enemy—my next thought was, "It's all downhill from here." I actually shuddered with fear and then tried to push the ominous thought from my mind.

My two little girls brought such joy to our lives. And Jason loved his sisters. We went to all his ball games—football, basketball, baseball. Jamie and Jill loved their big brother, and life was good. John was still working as a PE teacher and coach. In addition to my work at the hospital, I was teaching childbirth education classes and leading various Bible studies during the week. I added teaching aerobics to my increasingly busy schedule and got myself in the best physical shape of my life. John loved that.

The Seed of Discontentment

At some point between praising God and my many activities, I started to question the quality of my relationship with John. I had been twenty-one when we had gotten married, and he had been thirty. I'd changed a lot in nine years. He was the same. I tried to push negative thoughts out of my mind: "He's so boring. He never reads anything but sports magazines. He has no depth." But they kept returning. Deep in my gut, the first seed of discontentment took root. Sadly, I was not astute or spiritually mature enough to kill it. So it grew. That was my first mistake.

In the summer of 1983, I was relaxing and reading a novel. I almost swallowed my tongue when I read the words of the central female character that so perfectly mirrored my hidden thoughts. She said, "I knew it was time to get divorced when I kept daydreaming about becoming a widow." Ouch. Harsh, I know. But I realized that though I had never put those thoughts into words, I'd been thinking them. Occasionally, I would imagine what my life would be like if John were gone. I even went so far as to imagine the kind of man I would remarry. At the time, Tom Selleck came to mind. Of course, as a Christian woman, divorce was not an option, so my "innocent" little daydream took me to an "acceptable" place of change. A seemingly innocuous thought festered and grew.

Soon, my critical thoughts about John increased. I could not see any of his strengths—only his weaknesses. The poor guy did not have a chance against the perfect new life I was constructing in my mind. Up to this point, I had never considered divorce or told John of my discontentment. It was my private little secret, watered and fertilized by my active imagination.

My Christian friends started to notice something different in me—not just the fact that I did not show up to church or Bible study as much but in my demeanor. This chapter opened with one of their comments. I tried to open up to this woman, but she was so condemning, I thought. In reality, she was so truthful. Instead of turning to her for prayer and accountability, I ran. I ran from fellowship with Christians. And, most importantly, I ran from God. That was my second big mistake.

Now my daily quest was to plot my strategy to leave John. I told myself I could not be happy and live an authentic life with a man who saw me only as a trophy. While it is true that John cared about my looks, I'm sure he did see my value as a wife and mother to his children. I just could not see beyond his flaws. I'm so glad God can see beyond mine!

Once the cat was out of the bag and John became aware of the growing chasm in our relationship, it was too late. I had made up my mind. I believed all the lies you read in women's magazines and see on television—that an unhappy marriage will breed unhappy children. Blended families were everywhere. I rationalized, "My kids will survive. If we love them and don't put them in the middle of our issues, they will still have two parents who love them. Look at all the children with deadbeat dads—mine will be way better off than them." I believed my own lies as well.

Under pressure to save our marriage and feeling that I at least needed to show I was trying, I agreed to go to counseling, but my heart was not in it. Once when visiting the counselor by myself, he asked me, "What do you want to accomplish in your marriage, Danna? And how can I help you do that?" I answered, "You can help me get out of it. I just want out."

The details of our separation and divorce are not important. What is important is that you understand the insidious way discontentment grows, no matter what the issue. It begins with a thought, which grows until it is expressed, unless it is immediately squashed. I made my third mistake. I took action.

As I write this story in detail for the first time, I feel as though something has just grabbed my heart and yanked it out of my chest . . . again. Even today, I have remorse for dishonoring God and being so selfish. The divorce was more than twenty-five years ago, yet I can feel what James is admonishing us to do when we sin and grieve the Holy Spirit: "Come near to God and he will come near to you. Wash your hands, you sinners, and purify your hearts, you double-minded. Grieve, mourn and wail. Change your laughter to mourning and your joy to gloom. Humble yourselves before the Lord, and he will lift you up" (James 4:8–10).

The Consequences of Sin

In the years since our divorce, I have confessed my sins, repented, and asked for forgiveness from all who were hurt by my selfish decision. Yet, the consequence of sin lives on and is a constant reminder that when we disobey God's precepts lives are forever affected. God tells us how to live within his will for a reason. It not only honors him but also results in a better life for us.

The Lord gives us more than just rules to follow—he also gives us powerful illustrations of what happens when we don't follow his higher ways. King David is a perfect example. He had it all—power, wealth, admiration. In Acts 13:22, this is what God said about David: "I have found David son of Jesse a man after my own heart; he will do everything I want him to do."

David was a wealthy king with great power. He had everything, including many wives. He could have had any woman he wanted, but he wanted another man's wife: Bathsheba. So he took her . . . and he got her pregnant. Rather than stop there and take responsibility for his sins, he tried to cover them up. As a result, Bathsheba's husband was murdered at the king's command.

David was considered a man after God's own heart. And yet like all of us, he was capable of the most egregious of sins. As we briefly review David's fall, we must realize that we are not immune to the temptations of the world just because we are Christians. We *do* have the armor to fight the battle (Eph. 6:10–18). However, when we fail to put it on and succumb to sin, the fall can be devastating.

When we are caught in a web of sin and deception, it is extremely difficult to unravel our mess. Spiritually mature people can help us climb out of the muck and mire. Unfortunately, I ran from those who could help me in my time of rebellion. In David's case, God sent the prophet Nathan to expose the gravity of his actions and reveal God's prophecy of dire consequence that would follow him for a lifetime.

In 2 Samuel 12, we read the account of Nathan's encounter with David. At first he tells him a story about two men—one rich and one poor. The rich man had lots of livestock. The poor man had one sheep, which he had raised since it was a lamb and now was like a member of his family. When a traveler came to town, the rich man slaughtered the poor man's sheep and served it to the traveler rather than taking an animal from his own vast supply.

David was greatly angered when he heard this story and replied to Nathan, "As surely as the LORD lives, the man who did this deserves to die! He must pay for that lamb four times over, because he did such a thing and had no pity" (vv. 5–6). Nathan replied with these cutting words in verses 7–12:

> You are the man! This is what the LORD, the God of Israel, says: "I anointed you king over Israel, and I delivered you from the hand of Saul. I gave your master's house to you, and your master's wives into your arms. I gave you the house of Israel and Judah. And if all this had been too little, I would have given you even more. Why did you despise the word of the LORD by doing what is evil in his eyes? You struck down Uriah the Hittite with the sword and took his wife to be your own. You killed him with the sword of the Ammonites. Now, therefore, the sword will never depart from your house, because you despised me and took the wife of Uriah the Hittite to be your own."
>
> This is what the LORD says: "Out of your own household I am going to bring calamity upon you. Before your very eyes I will take your wives and give them to one who is close to you, and he will lie with your wives in broad daylight. You did it in secret, but I will do this thing in broad daylight before all Israel."

There is nothing more shameful than being caught in an act of sin. In his power and wealth, David had considered himself exempt from the laws of God. At this point, David could banish Nathan and ignore his warning, or he could humble himself and submit to God. This is what happened:

Then David said to Nathan, "I have sinned against the LORD."

Nathan replied, "The LORD has taken away your sin. You are not going to die. But because by doing this you have made the enemies of the LORD show utter contempt, the son born to you will die."

vv. 13–14

In his book *The Top 100 Men of the Bible*, Drew Josephs writes, "Though David had some major life failures, God made him one of the most powerful kings in Israel and brought the Messiah from his line. Though any man (or woman) fails, God does not desert him—that is as true for us as it was for David."[3] We know that God is faithful to forgive us when we fully repent as promised in 1 John 1:9: "If we confess our sins, he is faithful and just and will forgive us our sins and purify us from all unrighteousness."

David's immediate response to Nathan was one of conviction and confession. We realize the full extent of his repentance when we read his heart cry to God in Psalm 51:1–10:

> Have mercy on me, O God,
>   according to your unfailing love;
> according to your great compassion,
>   blot out my transgressions.
> Wash away all my iniquity
>   and cleanse me from my sin.
> For I know my transgressions,
>   and my sin is always before me.
> Against you, you only, have I sinned
>   and done what is evil in your sight,
> so that you are proved right when you speak
>   and justified when you judge.
> Surely I have been a sinner from birth,
>   sinful from the time my mother conceived me.
> Surely you desire truth in the inner parts;
>   you teach me wisdom in the inmost place.
> Cleanse me with hyssop, and I will be clean;
>   wash me, and I will be whiter than snow.

> Let me hear joy and gladness;
>> let the bones you have crushed rejoice.
> Hide your face from my sins
>> and blot out all my iniquity.
> Create in me a pure heart, O God,
>> and renew a steadfast spirit within me.

I cannot count the number of times I read and prayed that psalm in the years during which God finally brought full conviction to my heart related to my divorce. And after full surrender and true repentance, God restored me. He blotted out my transgression and made me whiter than snow. However, like David, the remnants of sin affected my daughters in ways I only wish I had known before my divorce. If we could see a movie of our lives from start to finish, many of us would make different choices. Sometimes we are so deceived by our own lies that we cannot see or hear the truth until we fall and come crawling back in humility to God.

In David's case, the prophecy of calamity upon his household was surely fulfilled. As Drew Josephs writes:

Not only did this son die, but David's daughter Tamar was raped by her half brother, Amnon. Tamar's full brother, Absalom, then murdered Amnon and started a conspiracy to take the throne from his father, who had to flee to Jerusalem. Only when Absalom was killed could his grieving father return to his throne.[4]

Like David, my family suffered dire consequences because of my choice to walk out on my marriage. I'm not saying that the prophecy of calamity on David's household is always the consequence of divorce. In David's case, there was bloodguilt as well because he had Bathsheba's husband murdered. In addition, in Old Testament times, David lived under the old covenant of the law rather than the new covenant of God's grace through the blood of Jesus. However, there are both natural and supernatural consequences when we ignore God's will. Despite the fact that we live under grace, God's moral laws are still of great importance. Malachi 2:16 tells us that God hates divorce.

We may consider our children innocent victims of our choices, but like David, mine were not spared from the ravages of divorce. That consequence alone should be enough to stop all of us from making the selfish decision to end a marriage because we are "unhappy." However, the purpose of this chapter is not to offer in-depth biblical teaching about divorce. It is rather to wave a red flag in the face of those of you who are making selfish decisions in your life and declare, "Be careful about your choices because they can deeply wound the people you love!"

God's Grace Abounds

I hope my story encourages and challenges those of you who would walk or run away from a marriage (or any other important responsibility such as parenting) and rationalize your action. That being said, some of you may be experiencing physical or emotional abuse. It is essential that you remove yourself from danger and seek wise counsel. But escaping abuse is not the subject of this chapter. I'm speaking of making life choices because you are discontent or unhappy. I can assure you that discontentment will continue to rear its ugly head—it did for me—until you face this issue spiritually in light of God's truth. Submit your life circumstance to God. He can and will give you the wisdom and strength to follow his precepts.

Before we divorced, I allowed John to come back for a couple weeks in the midst of our separation. It made me feel physically sick to give in to his demands, and I was angry. Yet, for a brief moment, I acknowledged to God that I knew he wanted me to stay in my marriage. As John walked through the door, I said a prayer, "Lord, you are going to have to do this. I can't." That was a good first step. But I did not trust God to do anything. I let my feelings win out. I was convinced that I did not love John. I was sure that my life would be miserable. Surely God did not want me to be miserable. That seed of discontentment had grown into an ugly weed that choked out truth. Two weeks later, John could not stand looking at my misery any longer, and he chose to move out.

I had no idea that my misery would transfer to my two beautiful daughters. The biggest regret of my life is that I let my selfishness poison their lives. Thankfully, God's grace does abound. Today, my girls love me deeply and even respect me. I am the first person they call when they have good news and the first they cry out to when they are in pain. I have fully received God's forgiveness, mercy, and grace.

Some of you would say, "It's time to forgive yourself, Danna." I would say, "No!" God's forgiveness is sufficient. I am living and thriving in the hope and joy of my salvation. But I never want to forget the price that was paid for my sin. It caused my girls much pain . . . it cost my Lord his life. God has given us a free will—the capacity to choose. Whether life "happened to you," or you created your own negative circumstances, you have a choice *today*. Choose to think and act in a new way, in a way that honors God and builds up others.

I cannot undo the past, but thankfully God can redeem it. I cannot take away the wounds inflicted on my sweet girls' hearts, but I can be a healing agent of God's love and mercy today. Whatever your issue, whatever your pain, God has an answer.

If you believe that God is who he says he is and that he exists in three persons: Father, Son, and Holy Spirit . . .

If you believe Jesus paid the price for your sin by dying on the cross and that he rose again to newness of life . . .

If you believe that the Bible is the inerrant Word of God and has all the answers to life's questions . . .

Then it makes sense that you would choose to live according to his truth rather than your own desires and feelings. Isn't it worth everything to give yourself completely to the one who knows you better than you can ever know yourself?

The central theme of this chapter can be summed up in the words of Paul to his younger protégé Timothy: "But godliness with contentment is great gain" (1 Tim. 6:6).

In the next chapter, we will learn how to honor God by walking more consistently in his Spirit and in the process gain love, joy, peace, patience, kindness, goodness, faithfulness, gentleness, and self-control. The reward is well worth the effort.

PART 2

discovering
a new path to
contentment

The Secret of Contentment

I know what it is to be in need, and I know what it is to have plenty. I have learned the secret of being content in any and every situation, whether well fed or hungry, whether living in plenty or in want.

Philippians 4:12

Content . . . satisfied . . . fulfilled . . . complete. Do these words describe your state of mind most days? If not, what must occur in your life for this to happen? Fill in the blank below with the first thing that comes to your mind:

I would be content if _____

_____.

Perhaps I did not give you enough space to write all the things you believe you need to live a contented life. A few years ago, I had my own laundry list of items that I was sure would bring me satisfaction. I was wrong.

Why Are We Discontent?

When I called out to God in my early twenties, fearing I was dying or losing my mind, I did not know how profoundly he would change my life. I had been struggling with bulimia for almost eight years and experiencing panic attacks for five. In the next few years following my new birth, I studied the Word, prayed, and surrendered my life to Christ. And I was outwardly transformed into a new creation when I trusted Christ as my Savior (2 Cor. 5:17).

As I already wrote, I followed the Lord closely for about eight years and experienced many victories. So why, when life was good, did I begin to lose my passion to follow Christ closely? The Bible says that as beloved children of God, saved by the blood of Christ, we have already been blessed "with every spiritual blessing in the heavenly places in Christ" (Eph. 1:3 NASB). Nevertheless, we live as if we are bankrupt at times, looking for satisfaction in things like work, family, experiences, or accomplishments. As you read in my story, I took my eyes off Christ and a daily dependency on him and turned them back on myself. Seeds of discontentment germinate when we put ourselves in the center of our world.

In this important chapter, I want to look at some reasons why Christians grumble, exclaim, or even desperately cry out, "What happened to my life?" Many begin to believe they are losers because they *should* have it all together. Some of us are struggling in just one area of our life and feeling guilty for that. Others may feel as if their entire life is a charade and are trying to "fake it until they make it." If you fall into one (or even all) of these categories, stop the negative thinking right now and move on to a more productive approach. You've already learned the importance of renewing your mind, so let's not indulge any more destructive self-talk.

What Do We Really Want?

The purpose of this book is to discover authentic passion, contentment, and joy, which are the overflow of a life surrendered to God. As I pondered, studied, and prayed about this subject, I sensed God asking me a blunt question: "Do you really want to learn my secret of being content, or do you simply want to learn how to get what you think will fulfill you?"

The answer to that question is essential because it will determine whether you are willing to yield your entire life to God's principles rather than follow the world's formula for happiness and success. We simply cannot have it both ways. I must shamefully admit that I tried to do just that for many years of my Christian walk. I rationalized and overspiritualized my motives and pursuits, thinking I could live effectively with my feet in two worlds. I would say that I cared most about being in the center of God's will, but in truth I wanted God's will to be in line with my desires.

The harsh reality is that we must choose whom we will follow and whom we will serve. If you are a true believer, you will not find deep and lasting contentment unless you follow closely after Christ. Sure, you may have a season or two that seem fulfilling, but if you are truly his, he won't let you live a lie indefinitely. He'll rattle your little world with trials and tribulations until you realize that life on your own is far too dangerous and deceptive. And lest you think you've arrived, he will most likely allow trials to test your faith throughout your life so you will never forget what you've learned and to whom you belong.

God wants all of us. Unfortunately, many of us don't want to give ourselves fully to him. If we are painfully honest, what we really want are the "benefits" of God. In *Habits of the Mind*, Dr. Archibald Hart quotes one of his favorite authors, Thomas à Kempis, who wrote in his own devotional book *The Imitation of Christ*:

> I had rather be poor for Your sake than rich without You. I prefer rather to wander on the earth with You than to possess heaven with-

out You. Where You are, there is heaven, and where You are not are death and hell.[1]

Dr. Hart says this about the quotation:

He is telling us to love God for who He is, not for His benefits, great as they may be. This leaves many of us in a dilemma. How do we separate His benefits from Himself? The answer lies in examining our motives and attitudes. As we lift our eyes off the benefits, we are able to worship God Himself with all our heart.[2]

Here's the defining question we all must answer at some point: Do I really want to love and serve God . . . or do I want him to love and serve me? If we are brutally honest, we all have mixed motives. Anything good, pure, and holy that flows from our minds or hearts springs from what God has seen fit to redeem and renew. We are wholly dependent on him for every good thing. That alone should give us hearts filled with gratitude and a desire to seek him passionately. I am convinced that God uses our brokenness (both before and after conversion) to draw us closer to him. When life is good, we are prone simply to forget how very good he is.

Learning the Secret of Contentment

Our key Scripture passage for this chapter, Philippians 4:12, reflects the kind of motive and attitude God wants from his followers. Let's read it again:

I know what it is to be in need, and I know what it is to have plenty. I have learned the secret of being content in any and every situation, whether well fed or hungry, whether living in plenty or in want.

Whatever cultivated Paul's perspective regarding his circumstances is exactly what we need to experience deep contentment "in any and every situation." We know from Scripture that he had his share of challenges, as he describes at length in 2 Corinthians 11. They include being in frequent danger of death, beaten with rods, stoned, shipwrecked, imprisoned, hungry, thirsty, and exposed to harsh elements. He closes by saying, "Apart from such external things, there is the daily pressure on me of concern for all the churches" (v. 28 NASB).

I think you'll agree that Paul experienced a few life challenges. So when he says that he has learned the secret of being content in "any and every situation," he really means *any* and *every*! Paul was not born wired for contentment. He *learned* it. And that is exactly what we must do.

Too often, Paul's next comment is taken out of context and claimed as a promise. He says in Philippians 4:13, "I can do everything through him who gives me strength." He does not mean that every plan he makes and every venture he pursues will be a stunning success. Sadly, too many of us have attempted to obligate God to a promise he never made in Scripture. Within the context of his message, Paul is simply saying, "God gives me the ability (strength) to find contentment despite my circumstance." Now *that* you can claim!

The popular magazine *Psychology Today* had an article in its February 2009 edition titled "Happiness, How to Turn It On!" *Ladies Home Journal*, in the same month, promoted on its cover "Feel Happier Every Day." Do these publications reveal the secret Paul spoke about? No, not even close. However, there is almost always an element of truth in writings about happiness and contentment.

Human beings have been studying themselves for centuries and have figured out how the brain works—the brain that *God* designed, by the way! The discussion we had earlier about changing the neuron pathways in the brain was "discovered" by scientists, doctors, and psychologists years ago. The power of positive thinking emerged from these discoveries because . . . it works. And it works because that is how God designed us. Even those who don't know God personally can improve their attitudes about life, diminish their negative thoughts, and increase their happiness by practicing some proven techniques. While there is nothing bad about these methods, they certainly don't draw one toward God. In fact, if they dull the pain of life, they often reinforce a person's supposed self-sufficiency. That's not to say I have stopped my deep-breathing techniques before I go on stage to speak or that I never take a bubble bath for relaxation—but they are not the real deal for discovering deep, abiding contentment and joy.

The secret Paul speaks about is available only to Christ's followers and can be discovered only when we are filled with the Holy Spirit and walk consistently by his power. Walking by the Spirit seemed like an incredibly mystical and complex aspiration before I began to study what the Bible has to say about it. What we must understand is that the Holy Spirit actually resides within *every* believer. Paul totally relinquished the reins of his life to Christ and learned to walk consistently by the Spirit rather than in his own power.

In Ephesians 1:13–14, we are told, "After listening to the message of truth, the gospel of your salvation—having also believed, you were sealed in Him with the Holy Spirit of promise, who is given as a pledge of our inheritance" (NASB). In Old Testament times, before the resurrected Christ sent the Holy Spirit to all believers, the Spirit would come and go depending on a person's behavior. In Psalm 51, King David cries out to God with a repentant heart because of his sin related to Bathsheba and his role in her husband's death. He says in verses 10–11, "Create in me a pure heart, O God, and renew a steadfast spirit within me. Do not cast me from your presence or take your Holy Spirit from me."

Today, the Holy Spirit does not leave us, though we can grieve him. Ephesians 4:30 admonishes, "Do not grieve the Holy Spirit of God, by whom you were sealed for the day of redemption" (NASB). From the moment you believed in Christ, the Holy Spirit entered you and will never leave.

Charles Ryrie teaches in the *Ryrie Study Bible*:

Sealing means the certainty of being possessed by God and preserved until the day of redemption. It is a guarantee of the Christian's security. Since Pentecost, all true believers are said to be indwelt by the Spirit which is a gift. Indwelling brings the presence of God into a Christian's life and anointing enables the Christian to be taught.[3]

However, being indwelt by the Spirit does not guarantee we are walking by the Spirit. Ryrie explains that being "filled" and "indwelt" are two different things. We are automatically indwelt at conversion. Ryrie explains that being filled is commanded in Ephesians 5:18 and means being controlled by the Spirit. He states:

> To be filled means yielding to the Spirit's control and though commanded, is voluntary and necessitates an act of dedication. This includes two aspects: initial dedication (Romans 12:1, 2) and continual dedication of one's life (Romans 8:14). Victory over sin in daily experience is necessary in being controlled by the Spirit. This means responding to the light of the Word as it is continually revealed. Believers may lose the filling but not the indwelling.[4]

Ryrie details the many tasks of the Holy Spirit in the believer's life, including convincing, convicting, interceding, inspiring, and teaching, to name a few. It's quite obvious that the presence of the Holy Spirit is not consistently discernible in our lives. If he is not prompting and prodding us, what is he doing? We can be sure he is convicting us of sin and bringing the Word of God to life in our minds. If we fail to fill our minds with the Word of God and quench the Spirit's promptings (1 Thess. 5:19) by leading a carnal life, we lose our sensitivity to him. It's as if the Spirit is dormant and we forget he is there.

Stirring Up the Spirit in Your Life

I once had a Bible teacher describe the power of the Holy Spirit in our lives using the analogy of chocolate syrup and milk. She said to imagine squirting thick chocolate syrup into a tall glass of milk. The syrup immediately sinks to the bottom of the glass. Is the chocolate in the milk? Sure. Has it permeated the entire glass of milk? No. It is on the bottom, available but not activated. Grab a spoon and stir it up, and the entire glass of milk becomes chocolate.

This simple example illustrates how we can be indwelt with the Holy Spirit without being filled or permeated. Without being filled, we cannot experience the fullness of his power working in or through us. We know the Spirit convicts us of sin and leads us at times. However, if we ignore his promptings and choose to follow our desires more than God's, we can quench his power in our life and soon become totally unaware of its presence. Fortunately, God allows trials and tribulations into our lives that can bring us back to a place of dependency and surrender. Then we are forced to realize our own inadequacy, fall on our knees, and ask, "How do I stir up your Spirit in my life and live in your power alone, Lord?"

As already discussed, the habits of our mind and life play an important role in how we respond to every situation. If our mind is continually renewed with truth and we consciously choose to set our mind on the things of God throughout the day, we are much more likely to walk by the Spirit rather than by the flesh.

The Battle between Flesh and Spirit

In my book *Change Your Habits, Change Your Life*, I wrote extensively about this endless battle. I think the teaching bears repeating here as we cannot effectively develop a heart of contentment unless we fully understand the war we wage every day.

"Flesh" sounds so base. But that is the word the Bible uses to refer to our humanness, or how we function naturally before God gets a hold of us. It includes our body and mind and the thoughts and behaviors that flow from them. Since the fall, man has fought against his natural inclination to pursue immediate gratification. As David Needham puts it in his book *Birthright: Christian, Do You Know Who You Are?* "We dare not forget that apart from God's intervention, flesh (mortal humanness) as such, functioning independently from God, has an unavoidable bent toward sin."

Before a person becomes a true believer in Christ, he or she can only follow one path of life—that of the flesh. Sometimes good and noble things are accomplished; sometimes not. But even the good things are done under human power alone and for their own gratification. It has nothing to do with God.

In the instant that you trusted Christ alone for your salvation, something miraculous took place—the Holy Spirit took permanent residence in you and made you a new person. And he is literally "jealous for you" wanting to have all of you, all of the time. And because he is constantly with you, you have supernatural power within you to say no to your flesh and to say no to sin. You have the ability to choose which path to walk: the path of the flesh or the path of the Spirit. Quite frankly, as Christians we make that decision many times (in fact, moment to moment) every single day. If you are not aware of those decisions, you are likely walking in the flesh. . . . This is the struggle that the apostle Paul spoke of in Romans 7:18–19 when he wrote:

> For I know that nothing good dwells in me, that is, in my flesh; for the willing is present in me, but the doing of the good is not. For the good that I want, I do not do, but I practice the very evil that I do not want.

Ever feel that way? I sure have, too many times to count . . . just yesterday! That is what happens when we follow our flesh. Fortunately, Paul did not leave us without hope. This is what he ultimately concludes with:

> Wretched man that I am! Who will set me free from the body of this death? Thanks be to God through Jesus Christ our Lord! So

then, on the one hand I myself with my mind am serving the law of God, but on the other, with my flesh the law of sin.

Romans 7:24–25[5]

When we allow Christ to become Lord of our lives, it is he (through the Holy Spirit) who gives us the power to walk in the Spirit. Notice I said "allow"—which is the willful act of submitting. When we believe in Christ, he pardons us from all our sins and becomes our Savior. But in the moment we are miraculously saved, we are not immediately perfected. We never will be this side of heaven. But it is God's will and our work to glorify him and allow him to transform us into the likeness of Christ while we are on this earth. When we walk in the flesh and seek our own gratification over his glorification, we cannot do that.

In my mind, I imagine two paths are always before me. One represents the path of following my flesh and the other the path of walking by the Spirit. Every waking moment, I must choose which path to take. Perhaps the following illustration from *Change Your Habits* will help clarify our choice:

Imagine for a moment opening up your door tomorrow morning and discovering two distinctly different paths extending from your front porch, each with a sign bidding you to come. The first is breathtakingly beautiful. Its smooth stones and lush landscaping draw you in. The sign says that you must travel on your own but promises to meet every desire of your heart. You feel quite certain it will bring you immediate pleasure. The other is a much narrower path, and you cannot see beyond more than a few steps. It seems barren and rocky, with nothing compelling you to take it. But the sign says that you will have a guide who has prepared the way for you and at the end you will find great joy. Which will you choose?

The first is the path of the world—the one that draws your flesh by promising to meet your immediate needs. It seems like the right choice. It feels right. Sometimes, the path of the world is simply the road you travel on your own steam. It doesn't mean that everything you do in the flesh is bad or immoral. It is simply done under your own power and for the purpose of achieving your own goals and satisfying your own desires. Those who do not know Christ can only walk this path. As Christians, it still tends to be our default mode more often than not. But, it doesn't have to be that way.

When we choose to "look up," surrender to God, and live out of love for him, this is the path of the Spirit. It is a path where both our motives and actions are pure and in sync with each other. But it's tough to stay on that selfless path; in fact, impossible under our own power. Some would have you believe that Christians can stay on the narrow path as long as they are disciplined and committed to God. This simply is not true. The "disciplined" walk is simply a "flesh walk" that looks spiritual. Walking with God is not a matter of discipline and commitment, it is a matter of surrender—choosing to walk in his powerful truth moment after moment.

God wants our constant thought and attention. When we learn to do this, we will always be on his perfect path. In the process, most of us will live a rather zigzagged journey as we traverse back and forth between the flesh and the Spirit. But it is a trek worth taking, despite our frequent failures, because our walk will get more and more consistent as we practice setting our minds on God.[6]

Before you can cultivate the habit of walking in the Spirit, you must make an important decision. Do you want to live to glorify God or gratify yourself? I guess I've asked the same question three or more ways in this chapter. The reality is, we need to address it each new day because born-again believers continually struggle with the choice to serve God or to serve self.

When I began to study the subject of walking in the flesh versus walking by the Spirit, I felt like screaming, "Just tell me what to do! *How* do I walk by the Spirit?" I'm still learning the complete answer to that question, but God has shown me in his Word what our part is in this supernatural process.

Paul says a lot about this mysterious walk. He writes in Galatians 5:16, "But I say, walk by the Spirit, and you will not carry out the desire of the flesh" (NASB). This is an exciting statement because it demonstrates a power beyond ourselves that can move us from our default mode of self to a new setting locked into the power of Christ in our lives. Charles Ryrie defines walk this way: "to take each step of the Christian life in dependence on the Spirit and to have victory over the flesh and its works."[7]

When we are dependent on God for each step we take, we are mindful of every thought and action. Like Peter, who walked on water as long as he kept his eyes on Christ and began to sink when he did not, we must keep our eyes on Christ as well. Paul expresses the battle we all feel from time to time when he continues in Galatians 5:17: "For the flesh sets its desire against the Spirit, and the Spirit against the flesh; for these are in opposition to one another, so that you may not do the things that you please" (NASB).

Our flesh drives us toward behaviors we should avoid, but we fail because our thoughts and attitudes have not been renewed by truth. Walking by the Spirit means we are submitted to and empowered by God's Spirit and Word. Paul gives us the really good news in verses 22–23, where we discover that walking by the Spirit has some positive benefits: "But the fruit of the Spirit is love, joy, peace, patience, kindness, goodness, faithfulness, gentleness, self-control" (NASB).

Think back to a time when you were completely relying on God to get you through a rough patch and sensed his power sustaining you. Do you remember experiencing his peace? Have you encountered a time when you seemed to have supernatural self-control or responded with uncharacteristic gentleness to someone who was being unkind or rude? Did you easily forgive someone who had wronged you greatly and surprise yourself in the process? Chances are in those moments you were walking by the Spirit. The fruit of the Spirit, however, is not distributed as individually picked attributes that God gives you just for the situation at hand. Rather, they all manifest at once (whether you realize it or not), and their outward expression brings glory to God.

Unfortunately, most of us fall on our knees and fully surrender to God only when we are experiencing difficult circumstances and feel we have no control. But the biblical teaching about walking by the Spirit does not tell us that this practice is for emergencies only. We need to learn to have the same dependency on God even when things seem great. If we can learn to have more of those moments all day long, each and every day, in good times and in bad, we'll be amazingly fruitful children of the King! We'll also be supernaturally content.

Walking by the Spirit

When as a Christian you do not allow God to meet your needs, three problems are created:

1. You are always disappointed with the results, no matter how well things go.
2. You will lack the inner resources you need to love others the way you should and to confront life successfully.
3. You will almost always be hurt and offended by the one in whom you invested all your trust, because that person cannot possibly meet your deepest needs.

So let's get to the bottom line of how to walk by the Spirit. God does the most important work when you come to a saving faith in Christ and he seals you with the Holy Spirit. If you are not absolutely sure that you are a born-again believer, then I encourage you to go to page 280 right now and prayerfully read about how you can know Christ as your personal Savior.

After the Holy Spirit is within you, your role is to:

1. Pray that God will help you surrender your entire life to his glory and help you choose the path of the Spirit more and more.
2. Consciously set your mind on God and his Word—not just during your quiet time or when you are experiencing pain or difficulties but all day long.

3. Fill your mind with God's Word so the Holy Spirit can bring it to life in your mind as you need it.
4. Become more mindful of your thoughts and what path you are on throughout the day.
5. Reset your mind and change paths every time you realize you are walking in the flesh.

God honors our efforts to seek him and follow him more fully. When we humbly pursue him with a surrendered heart and a desire to glorify him, he shows us the way. The path of the flesh is a lonely one. But when you choose the path of the Spirit, you are never alone and you are empowered in an exciting way.

In his book *Ruthless Trust*, Brennan Manning gives us an important perspective we must embrace if we are to live victoriously on this fallen planet. He writes:

> Jesus assured us of two things: presence and promise—Christ in you now and the hope of glory down the road (heaven). He never guaranteed that we would be spared suffering or victimization by evil-doing; in fact, he said flatly, "In the world you will have trouble" (John 16:33). What he promised was during our desolate hours there would be one set of footprints (Jesus carrying us). In varying degrees, suffering and loss touch every life—as does the presence of God in Christ if we have faith in his presence and hope in his promise.[8]

Paul learned the secret of contentment. It is walking by the Spirit. There we experience love, joy, peace, patience, kindness, goodness, faithfulness, gentleness, and self-control even when life is painful or disappointing. Like the labor of life we talked about in chapter 1, walking by the Spirit causes us to keep our eyes on the prize of heaven rather than on the pain of earth. It constantly reminds us that we will have perfect bodies, relationships, and lives one day very soon in the very presence of the King of Kings.

Walk a Mile in My Pumps

Shoulder to shoulder; hip to hip,
We'll get through it together if we don't quit.

Purse to purse and pump to pump,
We'll hurdle the hurdles and jump the jumps.

Head to head and heart to heart,
I'll show you the way; I'll help you start.

I'll show you the way over life's big humps;
Come along, my friend . . . walk a mile in my pumps.

Danna Demetre

It's been said that to understand another person well, we must walk a mile in their shoes—that is, understand life from their perspective. It is even better to walk in the shoes of those who have faced difficult life circumstances and emerged stronger and more whole. In this chapter, you will get a chance to walk a mile in several women's pumps, learn about their life trials, and most importantly hear how they moved from victim to victor by applying life-changing truth to their lives.

Role Models

As a little girl, did you ever notice an exceptional woman and think, "I want to be just like her when I grow up"? For most women, our key role model is our mother. If your mother is like mine, you are richly blessed.

She deposited many valuable treasures into my heart that resonated in me even when I was not living in sync with my core values. Her love, acceptance, and words of encouragement told me that I had worth and mattered. When I was at my lowest low, I somehow knew that I was loved and had a purpose in life. Her modeling gave me hope, resilience, and strength.

My mom, Mary Lou, has always been known for her great joy for life. I sometimes forget that she lives in chronic pain because she rarely mentions it. At about thirty-nine years old, she sneezed so hard that something popped, and she has had numbness and pain on her left side ever since. She was tested for years and the doctors never could figure out what happened, so she just moved on. Today, at almost eighty, she has a loving, joyful spirit despite the fact that her pain has increased immensely. When we spend a lot of time together, I can see the pain in her face and that she puts ice on her shoulder several times a day. I recently asked her if the pain ever gets intolerable. She said there are times when all she can do is pray, and that's what she does. She sets her mind on things above and on the promise that she will have a completely perfect and pain-free body in heaven one day. She said, "You just have to go on with life and live through it. I modify my activity, do what I can, and take a break if I must." (She's amazingly active; even with pain and numbness, she skied until she was seventy-two!) "So I've got pain. We've all got something. I can't really say that I'm content with the pain but rather that I am resigned to it. But I am content with my life and trust God to get me through."

Mom said her favorite verse is, "Rejoice in the Lord always. I will say it again: Rejoice!" (Phil. 4:4). When she had a mastectomy at fifty-six, she approached the diagnosis and surgery as if it were a routine medical exam. She said that one day in the hospital she cried for a bit, and then she was over it. "There are worse things to lose," she says. Many years ago when we went shopping together, Mom stopped me in the middle of the store and asked, "Do I look a little 'off' today?" I told her I had no idea what she was talking about, and she replied, "Look at me. I forgot my fake boob, and I'm all lopsided!" Then she broke out laughing uncontrollably. That's my mom . . . my role model . . . my hero.

Observe and Imitate

In every area of life, we learn first by observation. From walking and talking to driving and shopping, we are trained by those who have gone before us. Who you are today is a reflection of whom you observed, imitated, and repeatedly mimicked (most often subconsciously) for most of your early life. The end result, positive or negative, depends on the character of the people who most influenced you. When we have poor models (and we realize it), we have two choices: to give in and become like them or reach out and find someone who inspires us to change.

As adults, the role models we follow are no less influential as we attempt to navigate the often-treacherous road of life in a God-honoring way. Yet too often we are like a lonely traveler trying to find our way in the dark. Even if we had great moms and models in our youth, we all must reach out both to mentor and be mentored in order to become all God has designed us to be. He created us for relationship and community, and we need quality people in our lives throughout our lives.

Years ago, I heard a successful man speak at a large conference and share his moving personal story. He told of his difficult early life, living with his mother and twin brother in a dirt-floor slum with almost no possessions and never enough to eat. Nevertheless, his mother encouraged him by saying he could be anything he wanted to be. He knew one thing for sure: He did not want to live his entire life in a slum.

As he got older, he was surrounded by gangs and drug dealers, but he kept his heart and mind focused on the dream his mother had told him was achievable. And sure enough . . . he made his way out of the ghetto and was living the life he had seen in his mind because of his mother's constant words. This experience gave him a deep passion for helping underprivileged inner-city kids, and he dedicated much of his time to encouraging and mentoring them. He would say to them over and over, "Remember OQP . . . OQP . . . OQP," which meant "Only Quality People."

He knew from experience that we become like those we surround ourselves with. Even in the worst of environments, he kept his distance from those who could have shifted his focus from "momma to homeboys." He knew this was a major key in helping young boys avoid the dangers of ghetto life.

With the exception of casual acquaintances, most people influence your life either positively or negatively. They are either pulling you up or pushing you down. And you are doing the same. If you are struggling to find joy and contentment, who is pushing you down by commiserating with you in your pain or telling you that life just isn't fair? Who is pulling you up by speaking words of truth and not letting you wallow in your discontentment or excuses? Spend more time with the latter.

Well-meaning people can set us on a dangerous course of self-absorption and discontentment by simply saying the wrong things to us over and over. If you really want to learn the secret of being content, start by removing the negative messages in your life. Of course, you cannot remove all the negative people from your life—some of them may be family! But you can begin to identify the things they are saying and doing that are pushing you deeper into your own destructive thinking. We all need what my dear friend Sylvia Lange calls a "spiritual Nazi"—that is, a mature mentor who is willing to give you a verbal spanking now and then when you feel sorry for yourself or lose sight of God's plan and purpose for your life.

Several women in my life fit the "puller-upper" category. I hope that reading their stories about how they processed disappointment and pain will help you reinterpret your circumstances in a way that will transform you into a person who can "consider it pure joy . . . whenever you face trials of many kinds" (James 1:2). It is my prayer that these women will enlighten you and encourage you to pursue the secret of being content—which is really no secret at all—no matter what life brings this side of heaven.

....

MARY'S STORY—ASHAMED

People who do not receive validation as children that they are significant and deeply loved will struggle to believe in themselves as adults. The gaping wound in their hearts can stunt emotional growth and leave a persistent, nagging question resonating in their soul: Do I really matter? The answer to that question is, Of course! But sadly, words and knowledge rarely fill them up. That void can create a sense of deep discontentment even in the best of life circumstances. The only cure is an extreme makeover of the heart . . . by its Creator. That is what happened to my friend Mary James.[1] What follows is her story in her words.

To be blunt, my life was an accident. In 1965, my birth mom was in college, and my conception was an unwelcome surprise. In fact, it's a miracle that I even exist because her mother (my grandmother) encouraged her to go to Europe and get a safe, legal abortion. Fortunately for me, my mother sought the counsel of a Lutheran pastor. He and his wife "just happened" to be praying for another child to adopt, and so before I was even born I had parents and a home waiting for me.

Life seemed fine for a season. I rode donkeys, danced in the rain, painted pictures, put on plays for the neighborhood kids, and always had a song in my heart. But somewhere in the midst of my joy, things became increasingly complicated.

My father was a dedicated shepherd to his flock. He loved the church and spent a tremendous amount of time away from home. Unfortunately, my mother dealt with her increasing loneliness by drinking. When I was ten years old, she took me into the bathroom and taught me how to be a bartender. I didn't understand her struggles at my young age and resented her for being drunk all the time. I felt alone and insecure . . . as if I were the parent rather than the child. I knew she needed help and told her I was going to tell my father about her problem. Sadly, she responded by saying, "If you do I will disown you as my child."

My response to her bad behavior and emotional manipulation was manifested in growing bitterness, rebellion, and self-destructive behaviors. Children don't know how to process pain in a healthy way unless it has been modeled for them, so I simply did what I instinctively felt—I lashed out, hurting myself even more in the process.

My adoptive parents taught me about Jesus and made it clear the kind of behavior they expected from me. But I never felt they truly loved me. They just wanted me to be "good." But like all humans, I desperately needed to feel loved. My natural reaction was to gravitate toward the only people who seemed to care about me—the kids from my neighborhood. They showed great interest in me, and I wanted desperately to fit in, so at twelve years old I followed along willingly with whatever they suggested. Just wanting to be accepted, I responded to their introduction to drugs and alcohol. Like mother, like daughter, I figured. I began to get a glimpse of why she numbed her pain the way she did.

During this rebellious time, my mother was diagnosed with terminal bone cancer, and I was sent to stay with my aunt in Oklahoma. I had no idea that Mom would lose her battle within one short year. When she died, I was not even allowed to return for her funeral. In fact, I was not allowed to return at all. My aunt told me my father blamed my brother and me for the premature death of his wife. The comment made me angry, but inside I believed it to be true.

My loser status was official. I was tall and awkward, my peers constantly made fun of me, and I bought into the lie that I had helped my mother die. Words are powerful and stick with us a long, long time. If we believe them, they can influence our actions profoundly . . . and they did mine. I began to party like a mad fool. I smoked pot before school, took speed before track practice, and did whatever I could get away with every night. Anything that would shut out the pain of life or make me feel loved (even for a moment) was what I pursued. The silver lining in this time of confusion and rejection was that I discovered a love for country music and my gift of singing. Much later, I came to realize that God would use this gift to heal not only me but also others who struggled with shame and rejection.

Well, things got much worse before they got better. I became a teenage runaway and lived with anyone who would take me in. I lived with shoplifters, a man who beat his girlfriend almost to death more than once, and finally with a woman whom I was told was some sort of escort. I never knew that for sure, but regardless of her undesirable form of employment, she showed me love. I think she wanted to protect me from ending up like her. During my short time with her and her two children, I finally got back on my feet.

My father remarried, and he and his new wife asked me to return to San Diego. At first I tried to clean up my act, but before long I fell back into my old ways. My weight dropped significantly due to excessive drug use, and I felt like they did not even notice how much pain I was in. I finally walked into my parents' room one day and said, "I am self-destructing in front of your eyes and you don't even seem to notice." Somehow, I mustered up enough courage to seek help. Shortly after that I told them I was not going to step foot back in church until I personally desired to be there. I was nineteen at the time, and apart from a few Christmas and Easter services, I didn't go back to church again until I was thirty-four years old.

During all this time, I had been curious about my birth parents but did not feel a great need to find them. However, God had a different plan. I was miraculously reunited with them, and I am still very close to both of them today. Meeting them answered many questions, but it did not take away all the loss. It did not satisfy my insatiable need for unconditional love. In that quest, I ended up married at twenty-one and divorced at thirty-one but with two amazing kids—Tyler and Jessica. With God's help we continue to have victory over some tough challenges.

In the continual pursuit of "true love," I jumped right back into another relationship—but did not marry him right away. Drinking was a big part of our life. Sadly, I was oblivious to the example I was setting for my kids. Nevertheless, I managed to tell people from time to time what a great Christian I was. You see, I had God all figured out. I made him into who I wanted him to be, and I excused myself from following any of the rules in the Bible that I did not like, because, after all, I was a victim who deserved leniency. Today I consider them guidelines for fulfilled living.

One New Year's Eve, God met me on the bathroom floor. After another night of drinking that left me lonely and miserable once again, I came to the deep realization that life without God at the center would always lead me right back to where I was . . . empty, wounded, selfish, bitter, and nowhere.

My boyfriend, Dan (now my husband), and I split up, and I began to respond to God's promptings. At the same time, God was working on Dan's heart, and we eventually began looking for a church home together. A co-worker invited Dan, the kids, and me to a program that shared the message of salvation.

As I sat there listening to the Good News, I was incredibly moved by the message of hope and truth. I knew the "facts" the pastor was sharing:

> God loves us incredibly, but he is also perfect and holy and cannot look upon our sin. All of us have sinned and fall short of his glory. The price for sin is separation from God and death. But the free gift of God is eternal life through Christ Jesus. Jesus is the Son of God, actually God in the flesh. He was with God from the beginning, and he came to earth in the form of a man. He is all God and all man. And he was the one and only man who ever lived the perfect life. Because he never sinned in any way, he could be the perfect sacrifice for the sins of all humankind—past, present, and even future.

Even though I knew all these things in my head, that night they finally hit my heart, and I knew God was speaking directly to me through the pastor's words. Now I heard the truth of the gospel— Jesus Christ loved *me* so much that he died for my sins . . . *Mary's* sins! By *believing* this and understanding that there was nothing I could do except believe in Christ alone for my salvation, I could be saved. He had done it all . . . for *me*!

At the end of the message, I stood up and gladly went forward in response to the invitation to receive Christ as my Savior. When I turned around, I realized that Dan and the kids had made the same decision.

Our lives radically changed that night. For me, the blame game had ended. I was suddenly face-to-face with the reality that all my bad decisions and poor choices were mine, and I was so ashamed. What had I done? I knew Jesus had paid the price for my sins, but I could not seem to let go of the shame. When I refer to shame, I am not talking about healthy shame or the kind of guilt that causes one to ask for forgiveness, repent, or make amends with someone. I am talking about toxic shame, the kind that says, "You're stupid; you've ruined everything. You really are a mistake, and because of your choices God will never use you. Your life might as well be over!"

My past once again began to hold me captive, and I believed I would never be accepted or loved if people knew the truth. Thankfully, God in his grace wanted to give me not only eternal life but also a new life here on earth. Early in my walk with Christ, he led me to an event at which women were given the opportunity to come to the altar with their issues, such as believing they were worthless, pain and shame from abortion and adultery, and struggles with suicidal thoughts, eating disorders, or sexual abuse. All the shameful, ugly things that we can do or have done to us were mentioned, and much to my surprise, many of the women at the altar were the ministry leaders in the church. These ladies were willing to come forward in their brokenness, and because of that God used them effectively and powerfully in the lives of others. This experience gave me freedom from the past and hope for the future. I finally understood who I was in God's eyes, and that was all that mattered. Second Corinthians 12:9–10 says, "'My grace is sufficient for you, for my power is made perfect in weakness.' Therefore I will boast all the more gladly about my weaknesses, so that Christ's power may rest on me. That is why, for Christ's sake, I delight in weaknesses, in insults, in hardships, in persecutions, in difficulties. For when I am weak, then I am strong."

Yet, I wanted to believe I could do something to correct all the wrong I had done. I felt there needed to be a punishment to make things right. It reminded me of the scene from *The Mission* in which Robert De Niro's character felt so bad about what he had done and the people he had killed (including his own brother) that he tied a heavy load of garbage around his body. He proceeded to travel with a group of missionaries up and down steep, rugged terrain with that load of trash tied around him. When he came face-to-face with the natives, the ones he had intended to hurt in the past, they just walked up, cut the baggage away, and let it fall into the river below. They accepted his repentance, and they loved him in return.

As I began to embrace the love and forgiveness God so graciously gives, I realized that his love was not intended to be one-sided. He was calling me to impart that same love and grace to others. If Jesus says, "Go love the person who talked behind your back. Go love your parents even though they broke your heart. Forgive the person who violated you. Forgive the person who lied to you. Don't talk about your enemies but pray for them instead," that is exactly what I need to do.

God's Word brought me powerful truth and healing. And obedience to his Word brought me new power and purpose. I was especially affected by Galatians 5:13–15 as it is written in Eugene Peterson's paraphrase:

> It is absolutely clear that God has called you to a free life. Just make sure that you don't use this freedom as an excuse to do whatever you want to do and destroy your freedom. Rather, use your freedom to serve one another in love; that's how freedom grows. For everything we know about God's Word is summed up in a single sentence: Love others as you love yourself. That's an act of true freedom. If you bite and ravage each other, watch out—in no time at all you will be annihilating each other, and where will your precious freedom be then? (Message)

God has shown me not only how his love can free me from my past but also how he can heal relationships that many would say are irreparable. Today my biological and adoptive families spend holidays together. I am thankful that God placed me in a home, despite the challenges, where I was taught about Jesus. And despite the fact that I was formerly angry toward my birth mother for giving me away, I am now deeply grateful that she gave me life. God has given me a new perspective.

Are you living in this kind of freedom, or do you have a relationship that needs some healing? Are you willing to let go of the past and let Jesus Christ rewrite your life story? Like me, you may have some baggage that you refuse to release because your pride says you need to be the one to pay the price. None of us (even those you consider "good") is worthy of the love Jesus offers, but he gives it to us anyway. He is made strong in your weakness, and he alone can set you free from the past.

SYLVIA'S STORY—CHILDLESS

Those of us who've had children without the struggle of infertility or other circumstances blocking our way cannot fully appreciate what it is like for a woman who desperately wants a child and finally realizes she must let go of the hope once and for all. Think about the one thing in your life you desired deeply but never received. Whether it is letting go of a career aspiration or losing the love of your life . . . letting go is hard. My dear friend Sylvia Lange shares how she dealt with the harsh reality that she would never bear a child.[2]

"When I grow up I want to have a husband and children who adore me as much as I adore them." These were the heartfelt words of a ten-year-old recorded in her diary on April 11, 1970. That child was me. The entries that followed that year and in the years to come all included notes about how much I wanted to be a mom. I finished school and went on to pursue a career in business, where I experienced a great deal of success, but the truth was the only real achievement my soul yearned for was to be a mom. I feverishly dated, looking for a man to share my life with, and yet the years rolled on with no husband and no child. My twenties and thirties flew by as I watched my friends get married and raise children, and yet none of it happened for me. I went through a phase in my thirties when I considered adopting a child on my own, but over time it became clear that it wouldn't be the right choice for my life. What was wrong with me? Why did everyone else seem to get their dream and not me?

At the end of my thirty-ninth year, I met God, or rather, God met me. Through a personal crisis and the help of some people I barely knew, I began a relationship with Jesus Christ that eclipsed any relationship I had ever pursued with an earthly man. I stopped dating for a while and focused on getting to know this Man who had entered my life so explosively. My love for him and my hunger to know him overtook my world, and one day in my early forties, I woke up and realized that even if I never found a husband, I was truly going to be okay, for my life had become rich and abundant, as Jesus had promised it would.

However, not because I earned or deserved it, God did bring a special man into my life, and at the age of forty-one, I was married for the first time. My husband was several years older than I, yet he expressed a willingness to have a child with me, as he knew how important this had been to me. I know women are regularly having children at more advanced years than in generations past; however, when I looked at our life and my husband's age and extended it out twenty years, it became clear to me that this was not the right path for our life. I loved him too much to ask him to make such a huge commitment that would extend into his senior years. Suddenly I realized I was honestly and truly, cross-my-heart okay with that decision. And our life is very good.

Not long ago, someone asked me if I had become content with the fact that I never had a child. Remember, I had wanted to be a mom in the worst way, yet it never came true for me. I had to think for a moment before I answered. I realized I could not honestly say I was content. But what I could say was that I was in full *agreement* with God concerning his choice for my life. Today I get it. Today I see why he withheld this dream of mine, and I accept and embrace the life he gave me in exchange. Acceptance truly is the key to my own peace.

When our lives turn out differently than we planned and dreamed, we have a choice about how we will respond. We can get bitter as we continue to walk "in the flesh," allowing the years to pass by as we live in disappointment, somehow believing we lost out. Or we can learn to accept life on God's terms and walk "in the Spirit," actually behaving as if we truly trust that he loves us and understands what's best for us. Only then can we move forward in living the abundant life Jesus promised for all of us.

....

Diana's Story—Single

As you can calculate from my story, I've been married more than thirty-five years of my life. Thankfully, my second marriage is now in its twenty-fifth year and going strong. Quite honestly, I cannot remember what it is like *not* to be married. If you are over thirty-five and single, you probably hate me for saying that. We married girls can't always totally relate to single women. Truthfully, we sometimes envy you for the freedom your life represents to us. It's that "grass is always greener" mentality. Don't get me wrong, most of us love our husbands. We just look at your singleness from a different perspective than you do. My friend Diana Twadell helped me understand long-term singleness and offers a balanced and refreshing perspective about the hunt for Mr. Right.[3] Married or single, you will love her story!

"It's good that you still have hope." That comment, made by someone I had just seen for the first time in ten years, flashed in my mind when Danna asked me to share some thoughts about singleness for this book. I was at a women's event when I ran into this woman. We went through all the usual catch-up questions and answers. We had gone on a mission trip together in 1994, when we were much younger and both still single. She shared with me how things were going with her husband, two children, and ministry. When she asked if I had married, I said no, not yet, but that I was confident Prince Charming was still out there somewhere. Her response was, "It's good that you still have hope."

What was undoubtedly intended as encouragement came off as pity. But as a forty-four-year-old single woman who has never married, I'm past being insulted by comments like that. In fact, I find them kind of humorous. Most people, women in particular, think of singleness as "doing time until I get married." We live in a kind of holding pattern until we find our mate. We wait for Mr. Right like we would wait for a doctor's appointment—sitting in the waiting room, distracting ourselves with whatever's available, waiting for someone to call our name. Our focus is on how we got here, and our perspective is limited to our condition and what it will take to "get over it." But singleness is not a sickness. It's not something we have to get over. I've learned that my purpose in life is in the here and now, not in the somewhere and someday. It's important to plan and dream, but it's even more important to live and experience. The challenge, however, has been to live and experience *my* life, not someone else's view of what my life should be.

A few years ago I went to Hawaii with a couple of girlfriends. It was my first trip there, and we had a wonderful time. One of the issues I had to deal with, however, was *the bathing suit.* I don't look good in a bathing suit, and I am rather self-conscious. I knew I couldn't compete with the bikini-clad women I anticipated would be lying around the pool. But I remember thinking to myself, "You're going to Hawaii, and a large part of the fun of Hawaii involves a bathing suit. Are you going to sit on the sidelines feeling sorry for yourself, or are you going to jump in the water?" I decided to jump in the water.

I'm pleased to say no one shrieked in horror when they saw me in my bathing suit. No one pointed and stared and compared my measurements to the girls in the bikinis or made me feel inadequate. The truth is that most of us were too busy having fun in the water to pay much attention to each other's appearance. Our focus was on the experience, not the impression we were making or how we measured up.

So often we singles sit on the sidelines rather than jumping in the water. Instead of being intimidated by bikinis, we're intimidated by couples. I confess I avoided more than one company Christmas party because I didn't have a date. The same goes for weddings or other date-oriented functions. But then I once saw a dear girlfriend of mine at a party . . . with another girlfriend. They were having a blast. I didn't think, "Oh, how sad that Susie had to bring a girlfriend instead of a real date." I thought, "Hey, I wish I would have thought of that. They're having a great time!" I have since attended many functions with a friend that I might otherwise have skipped. And I even attended a company Christmas party alone. In every case, once I got to the event, my focus was on having fun and making new friends, not on the fact that I wasn't with my dream date.

Remember, "This is the day the LORD has made; let us rejoice and be glad in it" (Ps. 118:24). So go ahead and jump in the water! It may be a little uncomfortable at first, but after a few minutes, it feels great!

Danna shared in chapter 5 the importance of the apostle Paul's comment, "I have learned to be content whatever the circumstances. . . . I have learned the secret of being content in any and every situation" (Phil. 4:11–12). Did you know that Paul was *single*? I wonder if his friends ever asked him about his singleness? I can picture his co-workers talking to him at the watercooler: "Paul, you're such a wonderful man. How is it you've never been married? Are you dating someone right now? No? Why not? Where are you meeting people? You've gotta get out there, Paul."

Or maybe his co-workers decided that more drastic measures were necessary, like mine did many years ago when an envelope appeared on my desk containing the following ad cut out from a newspaper:

> Searching for a man named Russell who is 27–35,
> tall, and wears a size 12 bowling shoe.
> Voluptuous redhead is waiting.
> Call 500-1234.

Russell was the name engraved on my used bowling ball, which came with a bowling bag and size 12 bowling shoes, that I received as a practical joke from a college friend. I always joked that the bowling ball was my glass slipper, and I would try it on the fingers of every

Russell I met until I found my Prince Charming (or improved my handicap, whichever came first).

When my friends determined my quest for Russell wasn't moving quickly enough, they decided to expedite the process by placing a personal ad for me in a local newspaper. (This was before the internet was a popular dating scene.) Not only did they place the ad, but they also recorded the greeting on the private voice mailbox that interested "Russells" were directed to call. I've never sounded so sexy.

But despite their best efforts, only two "Russells" responded. The first was a part-time copyeditor and late-night deejay on the local college radio station who sported a goatee and a Prince Valiant haircut. The second wasn't a Russell at all, but he had responded to ten or twelve ads that day and couldn't remember which one he was calling about. Alas, the bowling ball remained in its bag.

A few years later, I had dinner with a married girlfriend who also happened to be a pastor. She brought up the issue of my singleness and asked if I was dating. I told her I wasn't really dating anyone at that time, and then she asked me why. I told her I didn't know. She then decided to hit me with the watercooler analysis. "Are you afraid of commitment? Afraid of getting hurt? Do you have some issues with your father?" It was incomprehensible to her that I wasn't dating *because I just wasn't dating.* Even more amazing to her, I was comfortable with it. Since she was a leader in our church, I mentioned Paul's words to her.

"Didn't the apostle Paul say he had learned to be content in all circumstances? Well, I'm content with my circumstances, and I'm trusting God for a husband. Isn't that a good place to be?"

She sputtered for a moment then answered, "Yeah, I guess it is." I don't think she believed it though.

As Paul said, becoming content in all circumstances, including singleness, is something we have to learn, and it's something that involves God. But learning to be content doesn't mean stuffing down our true feelings and putting on a happy face. That's denial. Learning to be content involves being honest with God about our desires and struggles and trusting him with our situation.

I didn't intend to be single at forty-four. Professionally, I'm at the top of my game as a partner in a large insurance brokerage. In fact, as I write this I'm sitting by the pool with a view of the ocean at a fancy resort on Maui on a business trip. I've also had some amazing ministry opportunities, writing and speaking to women, encouraging them to grow in their faith as I continue to grow in mine. And I've been blessed with a circle of amazing women friends to whom I grow closer each year.

We all used to talk and pray about finding the man of our dreams, and over the years I've had the privilege of watching each of them meet the man we had prayed for, fall in love, and get married. Except me. It's been hard letting them go, and I've had a lot of "what about me?" moments. And it's amazing how quickly "what about me?" becomes "what's wrong with me?" I have always struggled with my self-image, particularly my body image, since I've been overweight most of my life (hence, the bathing suit dilemma). But, candidly, most of my friends are carrying a few extra pounds as well (except Danna, of course). In fact, the only thing we've prayed for as much as love is getting our eating and weight under control. So my weight is not the problem. Are they prettier, sweeter, gentler, funnier, smarter, or sassier than me? Well, actually yes—in different ways. But I don't think that's the reason I'm single and they're married.

Here's my theory on my marital status: I don't know why I'm still single.

That's my response and I'm sticking to it—no matter how many times well-meaning friends and relatives ask me. I think one of the main reasons I get that question is that a lot of the married people I know are uncomfortable with my singleness because they're afraid I might be lonely. Comedian Mark Lowry shares a great story about going to dinner with some married friends. They too were concerned with his singleness, and one of them asked him, "Don't you ever get lonely?" He responded, "Sure, don't you?" The table then got very quiet. Of course single people get lonely. But so do married people. And just as marriage isn't an automatic cure for loneliness, singleness isn't an automatic sentence for it.

When people ask me about being single, I no longer get defensive and feel like I have to explain myself. I honestly don't know why Prince Charming hasn't shown up yet. But here's another true confession: About 80 percent of the time, I really *like* being single. And when I discussed this with a married girlfriend, she told me she liked being married . . . about 80 percent of the time.

It's amazing how often I focus on that 20 percent, though, and have found myself praying/whining, "Why am I still single, God? Why haven't you sent my mate to me? Why do I have to watch my friends get married while I have no one? Why? Why? Why?"

Over the years, as I have matured, so have my prayers. Now I say, "Lord, I'm struggling with my singleness. I'm hurting and I'm lonely today. Help me. Your Word says I can do all things through Christ who strengthens me. Lord, strengthen me to be content in the place you have me. You know I desire to be married, and sometimes it's really hard to be single. I'm trusting your Word, which says your grace is sufficient for me." (It's still okay to whine occasionally though. God can handle it.)

The desire to love and be loved is natural. God *created* us for relationship—with him and with others. At times, I have gotten my relationships out of order and have found myself "falling back" on my relationship with God when a relationship with someone else didn't work out. In other words, I "settled" for spending time with God on a Friday night if I had no one else to go out with. I shake my head when I think of the times I put God in the fallback position in my life when he is the only one who truly understands me because he's the one who created me.

God knows me (and you) better than we know ourselves. He knows our heart's desire to love and be loved. His words to Isaiah concerning Israel are true for us as well: "Your Maker is your husband—the LORD

Almighty is his name—the Holy One of Israel is your Redeemer; he is called the God of all the earth" (54:5).

I've found that when I've got my relationships in order—God first, others second—my singleness isn't a big issue. God designed me to be complete *in him*. Whether I'm married or single, I'll only find true contentment *in him*. Our relationship with God is the key to every other relationship in our lives.

Although I continue to grow in my singleness—living in the here and now, being honest in my struggles but content in my situation, understanding that my relationship with God is what's most important—I still wonder where my Russell might be. And I wonder if he's wondering about me. Lord, if it is your will that I marry, I pray you're preparing him for me as you're preparing me for him, and that he's growing closer to you every day. And most importantly, Lord, I pray he doesn't have a Prince Valiant haircut.

....

KRIS'S STORY—EXHAUSTED

When asked to describe her life in a nutshell, Kris told me recently, "I lived in hell without Christ the first forty-three years of my life. The worst day here on earth with Christ is better than the very best day without him!" Wow . . . that statement sums up the core message of this entire book. The question is: How did Kris develop this powerful mind-set? If you think it is because all her problems went away when she found Christ, you are mistaken. While she did experience profound healing from a life that included an alcoholic father, a mentally ill and suicidal mother, molestation, rape, promiscuity, excessive drinking, and an early marriage that ended when her husband threatened her at gunpoint, Kris's life did not become free of trials after she surrendered it to Jesus. After a three-year honeymoon with Jesus, she was literally knocked off her feet by chronic fatigue syndrome, which was so severe that she had to spend three years in bed.[4]

Yet it was in bed that she continued to study God's Word and pray until she became an amazingly grateful and beautiful woman of God. For another eight years, Kris had to carefully balance rest and activity so she could lead a somewhat normal life. Her fatigue and fragile health were always chasing her down and limiting her ability to live her life to the fullest. I met Kris during this time. You would never know to see her in public that she had any life challenges. The joy of the Lord exudes from her pores. She is funny, engaged, encouraging, and always full of joy. When she spoke at an outreach event for our Women of Purpose ministry, she had the women laughing their socks off before she moved into her personal testimony. Then they cried as she shared the reason for the joy within her and the hope we can all have in Christ—not just for eternal life but for peace, joy, and purpose each and every day.

The Lord miraculously healed Kris of her fatigue in 2003. Of course, she rejoiced greatly. Little did she know that he was giving her strength to meet some looming challenges on the horizon. When Kris's son Eric was twenty years old, he began to manifest bizarre thinking and behavior and was ultimately diagnosed with an array of severe psychiatric disorders. For the past eight years, Kris and her husband, Dave, have micromanaged Eric's life. He has endured three hospitalizations due to psychotic episodes, continuous trials of medications with their awful side effects, and continual dysfunctional and odd behaviors. They have grieved and been overwhelmed at times by the enormity of the situation.

Most of us cannot imagine the prospect of caring for our adult children for a lifetime, let alone dealing with an ongoing illness that manifests itself in grotesque symptoms. On top of this heavy responsibility, in 2007, Kris was faced with the reality that both her mother and mother-in-law were unable to stay in their retirement homes due to the level of care they needed and a lack of finances. Therefore, she moved them into her home, where "the girls," as she fondly calls them, are now happy and secure with their needs being well met.

If that wasn't enough, Kris also has had to care for her husband, Dave, for the past six months. A hip replacement two and a half years prior resulted in an undiagnosed staph infection that slowly grew into an abscess the size of a grapefruit. The problem was misdiagnosed for more than two years until the infection traveled into Dave's blood, and he became septic and very ill. After multiple surgeries and a long stint in a convalescent facility, he finally made it home and is recovering under Kris's loving care.

In those months of occasional email updates and prayer requests from Kris, her humor continued to shine through. She was always quick to give glory to God for the faintest progress and surrender to him when things looked bleak. As I prayed for her and Dave, I imagined her up early each day caring for Eric and "the moms," dealing with the bills, and shopping before running off to the hospital to encourage Dave.

When Kris and I finally caught up by phone, I asked her how she not only copes with the stress of her life but also remains so full of joy with her sense of humor intact. She told me she has her moments, and that sometimes a good cry purges the self-pity and pain. But for the most part, she simply takes one moment at a time and leans on the Lord daily for strength to meet her needs.

She has written something she calls her "Tool-Kit for Less-Stressed Days." Following are Kris's top-ten tools for dealing with life in the "stress lane"—not necessarily in order of importance.

#1: Humor

> A cheerful heart is good medicine,
> but a crushed spirit dries up the bones.
>
> Proverbs 17:22

It never hurts to look on the bright side and find something funny even in the most stressful times. One day when Dave was in the ICU and things were not going well for him, I returned home tired and very worried. I stood for a moment outside "the girls'" room wondering how I was going to muster up the energy for our bedtime routine. Just then, I overhead my mother-in-law (who has many maladies) announce to my mother (who had just broken her shoulder), "We should call this the home of fallen women." The laughter that night was enough to soften my worry and lift all three of our spirits.

#2: Prayer

> I cry out to God Most High,
>   to God, who fulfills his purpose for me.
>
> Psalm 57:2

Throughout the psalms we can read the heart cries of those who call out to God in their distress. The psalms show us that we need not be afraid to express our raw pain and heartfelt requests to God. They also remind us that God is always with us in the midst of our troubles and that when we humbly surrender our life to him, he gives us the wisdom and peace to endure each and every trial.

#3: God's Word

> Your word is a lamp to my feet
>   and a light for my path.
>
> Psalm 119:105

The only way to navigate out of the "stress lane" in this world is to steer into God's Word each day. There we can find truth that will equip us and light our way through difficult choices and circumstances.

#4: The Memorization of Scripture

Let the word of Christ dwell in you richly.

Colossians 3:16

I have hidden your word in my heart.

Psalm 119:11

In order for the Holy Spirit to bring God's truth into our life in a relevant way, we need to store up his Word in our minds so we can draw from it all day long. The memorization of Scripture was really tough for me at first, but it is well worth it. I love the fact that no matter where I am and at any time, I can gain immediate strength and hope from God's Word, which I have hidden in my heart. Bonus: It's a great brain exercise too!

#5: An Eternal Perspective

I consider that our present sufferings are not worth comparing with the glory that will be revealed in us.

Romans 8:18

This life is just a small dash in comparison to all eternity; it is simply a dress rehearsal for the awesome reality to come . . . heaven!

#6: The Practice of Contentment

I have learned the secret of being content in any and every situation.

Philippians 4:12

Too often I find myself wanting what I don't have, which reveals that I need more practice at being grateful for what I do have! God has blessed me with the gift of life. He also promises me eternal life because I have acknowledged that I am a sinner, repented, and trusted in Christ alone for my salvation. That alone is an awesome reason to be fully content!

#7: A Healthy Lifestyle

> Offer your bodies as living sacrifices, holy and pleasing to God— which is your spiritual worship.
>
> Romans 12:1

Our body is a gift from our Creator and our vehicle for this life on earth. If we don't care for it well, we simply cannot live out our purpose and will feel miserable, as if encased in a broken-down jalopy. We actually worship God by taking good care of ourselves. He gives us many instructions in his Word about how we can do this, including getting regular rest and renewal and eating right. To deal with the stresses of life, we need all the health and vitality we can get.

#8: Realistic Expectations of Others

> It is better to take refuge in the Lord
>   than to trust in man.
>
> Psalm 118:8

Perhaps by now you've noticed that we cannot control the people in our lives. They don't always do what we want them to do. Sometimes they make life difficult, or they anger or even hurt us. The Lord is the only one we can always trust to be there for us and always do what is best for us. This Scripture passage must be very important because it sits in the very center of the Bible!

#9: The Elimination of Stuff

But if we have food and clothing, we will be content with that.

1 Timothy 6:8

Have you ever noticed how much time it takes to care for your "stuff"? From knickknacks to clothes, the more we have, the more time and energy we invest in our material world. By scaling down and letting go of the unused and unworn, we can bless others and simplify our own lives.

#10: Simple Pleasures

Rejoice in the Lord always. I will say it again: Rejoice!

Philippians 4:4

Looking forward to even small delights can lift our spirits greatly. God has given us an abundance of pleasures on this earth to enjoy and to cause our hearts to rejoice in him. A few of my simple pleasures include a picnic on a grassy knoll overlooking the ocean, watching a sunset with Dave, a yummy frozen yogurt, a facial, and a fun night out with girlfriends. What about you? Whether you splurge for five minutes or five hours, do it . . . and rejoice!

KIMBERLY'S STORY—BETRAYED

You've most likely heard stories of women who were married for years to a man who they later found out was not even close to the person he pretended to be. I can only imagine the shock and heartbreak of such a discovery. Kimberly Scott was one such woman, and her story will not only move you but also encourage you to realize that God can walk you through even the most shocking and destructive of circumstances.[5]

I learned to love country music during some of my life's most painful seasons. Every song was my song. It didn't matter if it was about losing a dog, a best friend, or crashing your favorite truck. They all somehow resonated with me. This was especially true of a song by Rascal Flatts that says, "When life throws you curves, you learn to swerve."

Growing up in a Christian home and being raised by two amazing parents gave me a grounding that would one day sustain me beyond my wildest imagination. My folks were pillars of consistency. My dad was the same behind the pulpit as at the dinner table. His character was rock solid. My mom was always loving and spoke purpose, destiny, and value into my life every day.

Like most young girls, I dreamed of marrying a man who loved me completely. I knew this was possible because of the kind of marriage my parents had . . . and still have! I found the man I truly believed was my perfect match. And like my father, he chose to be a pastor. We had the privilege of starting several churches and even having a television ministry. We also had the incredible blessing of five beautiful children. Yet deep down I knew from the very beginning of our marriage that something was wrong. I always felt that I loved him in a way that he could not return.

I became used to living with his extreme mood swings, religious control, and anger. They became part of our lifestyle. I did not understand what was happening, but I complied with his wishes, hoping to diminish his dissatisfaction with me. My mom wisely said, "People surrounded by darkness can gain an appetite for shadows." I guess I just stopped seeing him accurately. My discernment shut down, and the darkness of my husband's behavior was blurred by my unwillingness to face the truth. My marriage continued to spiral downward.

Finally, the truth came to light when our youngest daughter, Grace, was only six months old. Through a series of discoveries, I was faced with the shocking reality that my husband had led a double life of active homosexuality since our engagement.

In an instant, I was stripped of everything in which I found my identity. Yesterday a pastor's wife and homeschool mom, now I was headed toward a new identity I never thought I would experience—a divorced single mother of five, unemployed, on welfare, physically and spiritually bottomed out.

Every aspect of my life was in shambles. Our home was in the beginning stages of remodeling and was torn apart—no floors, no water, no washer and dryer. There were holes in the walls, exposed wiring, and absolutely no security. My physical home was a pretty accurate picture of my life—broken-down and in disrepair.

I tried desperately to make the shambles feel like home, filling the holes with toothpaste, covering the cement flooring with carpet remnants, and painting the kitchen walls yellow to cheer it up.

My dad came over one day and showed me how to fix my walls correctly—doing it from the inside out and using the right tools for the process. Then he promised me that God would heal and restore my broken home and heart one day as well. And he was right. God gave me many powerful tools in my journey toward wholeness.

God's Word is our toolbox for this journey. His powerful principles help us turn our pain into purpose. I learned that by staying grounded in his truth and pouring out my heart to him in prayer, I can negotiate the past crashes of life, the present winding roads, and any future collisions I may face with courage and hope. I also learned that God gives us clear direction through his Word to help us navigate this journey well so we can reach our destination and know we have lived our life in a way that honors him and points others toward his life-changing truth.

One of the most powerful tools God gave me during those difficult years was from James 1:2–5, 12. For my own purposes, I changed all the "he and him" references to "she and her." This is how I read it:

Consider it pure joy, my sister, whenever you face trials of many kinds, because you know that the testing of your faith develops perseverance. Perseverance must finish its work so that you may be mature and complete, not lacking anything. If any of you lacks wisdom, she should ask God, who gives generously to all without finding fault, and it will be given to her. . . . Blessed is the woman who perseveres under trial, because when she has stood the test, she will receive the crown of life that God has promised to those who love him.

It became clear as I studied these verses and clung to others that there is definitely purpose in our pain. God helped me use three important tools found in His Word to grow and heal.

Tool #1: Wisdom

James 1:5 says, "If any of you lacks wisdom, she should ask God." I needed to pray constantly for wisdom to make wise decisions about separation, finances, raising my children, and simply surviving day to day. God gave me wisdom to show my children how they could have unconditional love for their dad and still maintain strong convictions about what the Word says about his sinful choices and their consequences. We were in a powerful spiritual battle, and the enemy wanted to undermine their faith and cause them to question what they had been taught as truth. I struggled with anger about my husband's choices but learned to turn it into righteous warfare for my kids' sake. God gave me the wisdom to realize that I should not raise my children to be haters of those who make ungodly lifestyle decisions or to become bitter because of life's difficult circumstances. He showed me how to raise my children to love people, discern sinful choices, and stand for the truth.

Wisdom comes from spending time in God's presence seeking him in prayer. The trials of life create a desperation that takes us to the end of ourselves and our own wisdom and into the arms of God, who is patiently waiting to offer his wisdom.

Tool #2: Strength

The second tool God gave me was strength. James 1:12 reminded me that if I was strong and persevered under my trial, I would receive a crown. And Isaiah 41:13 told me not to be afraid because God himself would strengthen me. "For I am the LORD, your God, who takes hold of your right hand and says to you, Do not fear; I will help you."

I needed both emotional and physical strength to raise five kids and provide for our entire household alone. In his graciousness, God plugged me into an awesome church family whose members loved us with all their hearts. And to add to that incredible blessing, they soon offered me a job as a pastor as well! I worked full-time for five years, and while I often fell into bed exhausted and spent, I never once got sick!

My job was so much more than a job, and I discovered that ministry was not just something that happened through a husband or a title. It is something God calls us each individually to do. In my case, he also provided income. God equips us to reach others from our own broken places and gives us the strength to do it well. He gives supernatural strength to accomplish his purpose through our pain.

Tool #3: Peace and Comfort

It is so easy to seek answers in the wrong places. Early in my crisis, I remember watching a Dr. Phil show in which he said that one way to achieve inner peace is to finish all the things you have started. So I looked around my house, which was a huge unfinished project, and decided to finish a few things that had been started: a package of Oreos, the other half of my *People* magazine, the stale bag of chips in my pantry, and a half bottle of Zinfandel. And I still did not find any inner peace. Of course not! Inner peace can be found only when you invite the presence of the Lord into your heart and living space. God does not always calm the storms of life, but he can keep us in the eye of the storm, where there is peace and comfort. Throughout my life, I had learned firsthand from my mom that we are able to create peace and comfort in our homes no matter how difficult the situation because we have the power to usher in the presence of God through prayer and praise. I made this my daily practice.

Praise music played a huge role in my journey toward wholeness. It lifted my spirit and helped me set my mind on things above. Even during sleep I could sense the presence of God.

Praying with and for my kids all day long sustained us in a powerful way and brought a peace and comfort that we all greatly needed. We prayed on the way to school, on the way home, at dinner, during homework time, and again at bedtime. As I spoke words about God's faithfulness—giving him credit for the big and small things he did—my children learned to trust him and know that he alone is our security. We can lead our families into complete dependence on the Lord by example, turning to him and audibly praying in all our times of need—no matter how small. When we consistently use the tools God gives us, a transformation happens from the inside out, and we experience some incredible blessings.

Trust and Hope

Women are known for overprocessing our problems. When we rely fully on God in the difficulties of life or when life is simply less than we'd hoped for, we begin to see things with new eyes. Proverbs 3:5 says, "Trust in the LORD with all your heart and lean not on your own understanding; in all your ways acknowledge him, and he will make your paths straight."

I learned to stop dissecting my life and trying to analyze all the reasons my marriage had failed and instead to trust God to give me "a crown of beauty instead of ashes, the oil of gladness instead of mourning," as it says in Isaiah 61:3. A divine exchange happened when I released the ashes of my life to God completely and embraced the beauty of his purpose for my pain. When I did, I could sense him directing my path. God alone is in charge of our journey. He is sovereign and will not waste a moment of our pain. He will use it to shape and mold us into his very nature.

We must lean on Christ on this road trip of life, and as we do, we learn that he is trustworthy. His wisdom and strength are poured out, and our trust and hope grow as we no longer fear the outcome of our circumstances. Christ does not fail us as some of our relationships can. Even close friends at times will let us down, but he is always faithful . . . always trustworthy.

Part of my journey out of pain involved letting go of my past hopes and expectations. I had always wanted to have a marriage that created lasting, positive memories. Such a hope grew out of seeing my grandparents' loving relationship. My parents were also building that kind of legacy. They had loved each other so long that they had begun to look alike, sound alike, finish each other's sentences, and even smell alike!

As I let go of that desire and leaned on Christ as my faithful guide in the ups and downs of my new life, I realized I was beginning to look and sound like him, responding as he would, finishing his sentences—as his Word permeated my heart and came out of my mouth. And the Bible says that I am actually the fragrance of Christ (2 Cor. 2:15), as his very nature and attributes surround me.

God's purpose through my pain was to help me profoundly realize that Christ is in me and constantly with me, directing and leading, giving wisdom, strength, and peace every step of the way. And all the while, I am beginning to look like the person who has been in the driver's seat all along: Jesus.

When we are squeezed by life, we can wallow in the pain or we can draw near to the one who can help us through it. I came to realize that I could have complete joy despite my circumstances, even if I stayed a single mom for the rest of my life. However, God in his graciousness chose to bring an incredible man of God (who had spent his entire adult life as a pastor) into my life. Tim Scott and I married on May 5, 2006, and he became not only a husband to me but also a much-needed father to my children. Today, my children range from seven to eighteen. I consider his two grown daughters my family and their babies my grandbabies.

Tim knew that our broken physical home symbolized our shattered life for a season, and so he made it his mission to transform it into something beautiful and new. It went from being eighteen hundred square feet of shambles to forty-nine hundred square feet of beauty complete with a pool, hot tub, and outdoor fireplace, not to mention a trampoline for the kids and a desperately needed washer and dryer for me. I am loved by my husband in a way I never expected to experience in my lifetime.

In our new life, God is giving us exactly what we need to be equipped to minister to both our own family and our church family in deep ways—much deeper than if our lives had always been as we had originally hoped. God is faithful and always reveals purpose through our pain.

....

MARILYN'S STORY—VIOLATED

When I think about all the atrocities that evil people do in this fallen world, I am most moved to righteous indignation by those who prey on children. It breaks my heart to imagine an innocent child being forced to see and experience things they should never encounter. Marilyn's story will move you deeply, and her journey out of the pit of hell will inspire you greatly.[6]

Multiple personality disorder. That diagnosis scared me so entirely that I wanted to run for my life—or, more accurately, *from* my life. But despite that ominous label and the reality of my emotional fragility, God held me tightly and walked with me through a refining fire that transformed my old life into a place of peace and joy.

You may wonder how someone becomes so broken that their personality fragments into distinctly different people. For me, it was a way of coping with a very dark and painful childhood. From as early as I can remember, I was sexually molested by my father, grandfather, and their friends—sometimes even in groups. *Incest* is a dirty, ugly word. Living it is even uglier.

After those gruesome encounters, I remember talking to God. He was the only thing that made my life bearable as a child. I really didn't know much about him, but somehow in my innocence I knew he loved me and was my friend. I turned to him in my times of need . . . over and over and over again.

Later, at the age of nineteen, I came to understand how I could have an intimate relationship with God through his Son Jesus, and I gave my heart to Christ. While my faith grew over the next fifteen years, I did not realize that I was still dragging emotional baggage from my past into my new life. As a wife and later a mother, I remained stuck in clinical depression and suffered from chronic anxiety attacks, self-loathing, and social phobias as I continuously struggled to recover from the horrific abuse of my childhood. I was desperate for God's transforming hand in my life.

God is not a personal genie, and faith in Christ is not a magic wand for all of our problems. I had received God's gift of forgiveness and the promise of eternal life, but I did not believe he had anything more for me. I slowly began to realize that I was not doing my part to fully receive and embrace all he had died to give me. I think in some ways I was waiting for him to bring all the promises to me on some kind of spiritual silver platter. I simply was not cooperating and taking responsibility for *my* role in *our* relationship. As I cried out for him to deliver me from the emotional oppression that was robbing me of the joy he promised, he began to teach me about active belief.

My anchor of hope and strength during my years of emotional oppression was a growing understanding that this God who had revealed his love and strength to me as a child is also a God of healing. This very same God, who committed himself to me in the midst of my darkest hours, is also the God who died for me over two thousand years ago on a cross. His name is Jesus Christ. Just as he carried my sins on his back, he will carry my brokenness on his back as well . . . if I release it to him. His death paid the just penalty for all my sin and began a healing process in me from the inside out, releasing me from my dreadful shame. I am forgiven and continue to be transformed day by day into a new person.

But to be honest, I don't always feel like a new creation. I remember one particular day when I was quite angry with God because he wasn't changing me quickly enough. Ignoring the fact that he had quite the task ahead of him, I recited back to him his own promise in his Word: "If anyone is in Christ Jesus, he is a new creation; the old has gone, the new has come!" (2 Cor. 5:17).

"Lord, I need an extreme makeover!" I demanded. "I mean from top to bottom. Please, God, dig it up and start over. I'm tired and I'm frustrated. I thought my new life in Christ would come more quickly and not be quite so expensive. I mean it, Lord. Why do I have to pay one hundred dollars an hour for my new life in Christ? After seven years of counseling, isn't it time for my new life to come? Why am I still in the emotional trenches of past wars? I am so sick of myself and my oppressive emotional pain. Please, God, make me over!"

You see, I feared that perhaps God's promises were for everyone but me. Deep down I had always believed I was unlovable. God's slow hand of deliverance in my life only seemed to confirm this lie grounded in self-hatred. Yet, God met me in my painful lies and began to teach me a profound truth that day. He showed me that the journey of faith is about building an incredibly intimate partnership . . . a profoundly personal relationship. In it, he does the transforming, but we do the believing. The believing is about taking the truths and promises from his Word and not just believing in my head that he said them but rather believing in my heart that he said them to *me* personally.

After I finished crying out to God, I went to my desk and reached for a pen and some index cards. Then I headed to my fireplace, where I opened a box of matches, knelt down, and began to pour out my heart to God, giving him every piece of me. Despite my frustration that God had not yet delivered on his promise, I was desperate for his healing touch on my heart and my mind.

"Okay, Lord, you are on!" I exclaimed. "I accept your challenge and trust you to do all the hard work." I believed he would give me grace for the journey. Kneeling at the fireplace with pen, index cards, and matches in hand, I was ready to write down, surrender, and burn anything God told me to get out of my life.

In those moments, God began to reveal insights about my alter personalities that I had not clearly understood before. I now saw them as extremely creative tools for surviving something no little girl should ever have to experience. Obviously, those alter egos had served me well for a season. I was able to earn a 4.0 high school GPA, was president of my class, and was even selected to participate in the state speech championship. I was also elected California Girls' State Governor. By dissociating from my pain and the harsh reality of my life, I had been able to maintain my secret and in some ways even hide it from myself. But deep down, those personalities had appetites I could no longer appease. My creative coping had turned on me, entangling me in a life of clinical depression, bulimia, suicidal ideations, crippling anxiety, many physical ailments, and confused dissociations.

Now in the light of truth, I began to write the name of each personality on an index card. On the other side, I wrote why I didn't need her anymore. For instance, there was Tera. I named her Tera because she was terrified of life . . . all of life. Tera was also the biggest of my personalities. When I would go into Tera, I would lose almost all sense of reality. God revealed to me I did not need Tera to carry my fear. He reminded me of a verse in the Bible, "Perfect love drives out fear" (1 John 4:18), and he challenged me to lean on his living Spirit to carry my fear, just as Jesus had carried my sins.

Then there was Joy. She was the part of me that could separate herself from an evening of appalling abuse and happily romp on the playground the next morning. But once again, a verse from the Bible came to mind: "The joy of the LORD is your strength" (Neh. 8:10). I no longer needed to dissociate to enjoy life. Life is hard, but the joy of the Lord is now my strength!

There were many more personalities to relinquish. I remained at the fireplace for hours, weeping and letting go of lifelong friends. I thanked them for all they had done to help me through, but I also acknowledged that I didn't need them anymore. I was moving on. I wanted to be whole. I did not want to be Humpty Dumpty in a million pieces the rest of my life. I was ready for the King to put me back together again! I no longer needed them because I had God's Spirit within to sustain me and hold me for eternity. I was trusting with all my heart in the words of Isaiah 53:4–5: "He [Jesus] took up our infirmities and carried our sorrows. . . . By His wounds we are healed." Did you catch that? We're not just forgiven. We are healed.

The healing we receive from the Holy Spirit living inside us is not only for the forgiveness of our own sin but also for deliverance from the sin done to us that entangles us and prompts us into more sin of our own. Shame and sin are cyclical. Sin begets shame and shame begets sin. Who will stop this endless cycle? Jesus holds out his arms on the cross and cries, "It is finished." As we reach out and take his hand, believing in an active way that his work on the cross was not in vain, we are healed from this degenerative life of sin. Victory over sin is a continual process toward life-changing freedom. In Christ alone we are truly transformed!

. . . .

The stories in this chapter reflect life circumstances over which these women had little control. Things happened (or didn't), and each woman learned how to shift her focus from pain and disappointment to healing and contentment. While all of our life situations are different, I hope you gained perspective and hope after hearing these stories. If these women can learn the secret of contentment, so can you . . . really! And I certainly hope that their accounts did not make you feel guilty or ashamed for not handling your life as well. You need to know that they *all* had their moments of discontent and still do from time to time. They just don't stay there for long because they have learned the power of walking in the Spirit.

The commonality of these uniquely different women is their spiritual maturity. Each will tell you that she doesn't take credit for the peace and joy she finds in the midst of life's difficulties. They all still must rely on the Lord every day to sustain them. As I've said before, and it bears repeating, none of us ever arrives this side of heaven. We are works in progress, and we need each other to point the way when our heads are down and we are too focused inwardly on our own troubles. Life is tough, but God is good. Hang on tightly to his hand.

PART 3

the forty-day journey

7

The Forty-Day Journey
to Rediscover
Contentment and Joy

Love the Lord your God with all your heart and with all your soul and with all your mind. This is the first and greatest commandment.

Matthew 22:37

The ultimate "one thing" that Jesus spoke of is summed up perfectly in the verse above. However, learning *how* to live out that command in the practical details of life is what this book is all about. When we learn to do this, we will experience contentment despite our circumstances. When Paul says in Philippians 1:21, "For to me, to live is Christ and to die is gain," we can hear the passionate expression of a man who has made the love of God through Christ his "one thing." He then compares everything else to that love and writes in Philippians 3:8, "What is more, I consider everything a loss compared to the surpassing greatness of knowing Christ Jesus my Lord, for whose sake I have lost all things."

Loving God with our entire being requires a daily decision to "look up" and follow God and trust in his principles rather than to "look in" and pursue our own immediate gratification. When we invest our time in studying God's Word, praying, and worshiping, we are storing up treasures in heaven that will never be taken from us. All the rest is simply "wood, hay or straw" that will ultimately be burned with nothing remaining (see 1 Cor. 3:12–13).

Trusting God and believing in his promises are crucial to discovering lasting contentment. Sometimes in our daily discomfort, we miss how the Lord is working within our circumstance to draw us closer to him. Growing in intimacy with him is the only way we can find authentic satisfaction. It is my hope and prayer that you will find a refreshed faith and renewed joy during the next forty days. As you approach each day with a surrendered heart, God will renew your strength of body, soul, and spirit. He will meet you where you are and take you so much higher!

> But those who hope in the LORD
>   will renew their strength.
> They will soar on wings like eagles;
>   they will run and not grow weary,
>   they will walk and not be faint.
>
> Isaiah 40:31

Our daily journey will include a devotional with each day's key Scripture passage coming from Christ's own words as recorded in the New Testament. You will soon notice that our focus is not solely on the subject of contentment and joy but rather on the wide variety of wisdom Christ imparts on many subjects. To become whole and holy, we need all of his words, not just the ones we think speak to us in our current circumstance. In fact, sometimes the Holy Spirit speaks to us in unexpected ways as we surrender our burdens and submit ourselves completely to his teaching.

After you read and ponder the words of Christ each day, you will have an opportunity to record your words of worship and thankfulness, confessions, and prayer requests.

The Lord's Prayer

It seems fitting to include the model Jesus used when he taught his disciples to pray as part of our daily walk. Within the Lord's Prayer, we discover important spiritual practices of worship, submission, petition, spiritual protection, and forgiveness. Let's read it in its entirety and then take a closer look at each area:

> Our Father who is in heaven,
> Hallowed be Your name.
> Your kingdom come,
> Your will be done,
> On earth as it is in heaven.
> Give us this day our daily bread.
> And forgive us our debts, as we also have forgiven our
> debtors.
> And do not lead us into temptation, but deliver us from evil.
> For Yours is the kingdom and the power and the glory for-
> ever. Amen.

Matthew 6:9–13 NASB

We know this prayer pleases God and directs our focus and requests in a way that honors him because Jesus told his disciples to pray this way. Let's briefly consider each aspect below.

Our Father Who Is in Heaven

We are instructed to approach the God of the entire universe as *our* Father, not as *the* Father or *a* Father. He is *ours*, and his home is in heaven—our future residence. It occurred to me that I often skip over this important salutation and miss its powerful significance. From the outset of this prayer, we remind ourselves that we are children of the King of all creation and should set our minds on things above.

Hallowed Be Your Name

We don't use the word *hallowed* in our daily language. I like that, because God is the only one who deserves such a unique word of praise. Authentic worship is one thing we can actually give to God. It gets our hearts and minds off ourselves and onto our Father—the mighty, glorious, all-knowing, true, and living God. In our daily journey, let us become excellent worshipers.

I felt deep conviction about how and what I worship after reading a beautiful little book called *The Air I Breathe* by Louie Giglio. In it he writes:

> Worship is simply about value. The simplest definition I can give is this: Worship is our response to what we value most. So, how do you know where and what you worship? It's easy. You simply follow the trail of your time, your affection, your energy, your money, and your allegiance. At the end of that trail you'll find a throne; and whatever, or whomever, is on that throne is what you worship. We may say we value this thing or that thing more than any other, but the volume of our actions speaks louder than our words. In the end, our worship is more about what we do than what we say.[1]

Most of us want to worship God in spirit and in truth. We don't want to be surface Christians who simply go through the motions. But if we are not seriously intentional, it is easy to do just that. My friend Sylvia (you read her personal story earlier) no longer calls herself a Christian but rather a devoted Christ follower. There is a lot of action in that description. Let's take action and be authentic worshipers of the only one who deserves our praise.

Your Kingdom Come

When we turn our attention to the reality that this earth will pass away and God's new heaven and new earth will eventually be our perfect home, we gain perspective about life on this fallen planet. To live a life of purpose, we need to remember what Jesus said in John 17:16: "They are not of the world, even as I am not of it." By keeping that in the forefront of our minds, we won't get so emotionally entangled in the things of this world—both good and bad.

Your Will Be Done

Just as Jesus prayed in the Garden in Gethsemane before he was taken captive, "Yet not my will, but yours be done" (Luke 22:42), we must constantly submit our desires to the greater wisdom of God. In his book *Ruthless Trust*, Brennan Manning writes, "The supreme need in most of our lives is often the most overlooked—namely, the need for an uncompromising trust in the love of God."[2] If we truly believe God is trustworthy and acts out of love for us, we can say with conviction, "Your will be done."

Give Us This Day Our Daily Bread

We finally made it to the request area of this prayer. Notice how short it is. I love the simplicity of Jesus's instruction to pray for today's need. In Matthew 6:33–34, he taught the people, saying, "But seek first his kingdom and his righteousness, and all these things will be given to you as well. Therefore do not worry about tomorrow, for tomorrow will worry about itself. Each day has enough trouble of its own." God holds the future in his hands, and he knows all of our needs before we do. When we put his kingdom first, he meets our needs . . . for today. This does not mean we can't approach God with all our burdens and concerns. But Jesus's example does help us see that our time in prayer is not just for asking God to intervene in our lives but for worshiping, confessing, and thanksgiving as well. As C. S. Lewis says, "Praying for particular things . . . always seems to me like advising God how to run the world. Wouldn't it be wiser to assume that He knows best?"[3]

And Forgive Us Our Debts

Our debts against God are called sin. We need to take a daily inventory of our "sin account" and present it to him so we can keep our life pure and holy. If we ignore our trespasses, we begin to become desensitized, like the frog in the pot that doesn't notice the water is slowly coming to a boil. However, "if we confess our sins, he is faithful and just and will forgive us our sins and purify us from all unrighteousness" (1 John 1:9). We need daily confession to wipe our slate clean and restore our fellowship with the Lord.

As We Also Have Forgiven Our Debtors

I always feel so much better when I submit all my failings to the Lord and ask for his forgiveness, knowing that he welcomes me with open arms no matter how badly I have messed up. Yet, this next phrase causes me to pause and ask myself, "Do I extend the same grace and mercy to others that God extends to me?" Perhaps we overlook Matthew 6:14–15, the verses that follow the Lord's teaching on prayer. This is what Jesus says: "For if you forgive men when they sin against you, your heavenly Father will also forgive you. But if you do not forgive men their sins, your Father will not forgive your sins." These sobering and convicting words will hopefully move us to obedience.

Do Not Lead Us into Temptation, but Deliver Us from Evil

God doesn't tempt us, but he does allow us to encounter situations in which our faith is tested and strengthened. If we fail to turn to God, we may give in to our own desires and pursue sin. James 1:13–15 tells us, "When tempted, no one should say, 'God is tempting me.' For God cannot be tempted by evil, nor does he tempt anyone; but each one is tempted when, by his own evil desire, he is dragged away and enticed. Then, after desire has conceived, it gives birth to sin; and sin, when it is full-grown, gives birth to death." Therefore, we include in our prayers a petition to be protected from situations that may lead us to sin, and when we are tempted, we pray for the strength to flee from the temptation and practice what we are taught in James 4:7–8: "Submit yourselves, then, to God. Resist the devil, and he will flee from you. Come near to God and he will come near to you."

For Yours Is the Kingdom and the Power and the Glory Forever

As we close our prayer, we end as we started by praising and acknowledging God and his ultimate plan. Here we can express our gratitude and thankfulness for God's sovereignty and provision today and always.

Daily Choices

When life is in its usual routine, where do you choose to spend your time? I have said for many years, "We make time for that which is most important to us." Of course there are days, weeks, and sometimes seasons when unusual circumstances turn our world upside down. But most of the time, we fall into patterns that don't vary much from day to day. Most of us have at least one or two discretionary hours each day that we can spend as we desire. We choose television or the Bible, worship music or our favorite magazine, a few quiet moments in prayer or more time chatting on the phone. Life is a series of choices. If we pay close attention, we can see that even the busiest among us fritter away little chunks of time.

In the next forty days, I'm asking you to carve out about fifteen to twenty minutes each day to read a devotion and write your thoughts and prayers. If you can take more time and read the Scripture surrounding the day's verse, or others that are shared within the teaching, that's even better! If you can't, I believe you will still gain a great deal from the daily exercise. If you miss a day or two now and then, just pick up where you left off. If the journey takes more than forty days, so be it. The objective is to find some consistency and make it to day forty!

As you will see illustrated below, each day includes a section where you can express your worship, confession, thankfulness, and prayer requests to God. In addition, you will ask yourself what lie you may believe related to the topic of the day and then what truth you think God wants you to receive instead. Before you read the devotion for the day and respond in writing, ask the Lord to open your mind and heart to what he wants to do in your life that day. Then after reading, begin writing. I highly recommend finding time each morning to begin your day with the Lord. If you don't finish, take your book with you for the day—or spend a few minutes at the end of the day writing and reflecting on what God has taught you.

During this time each day, be as honest and real as you can. Don't be afraid that you will make mistakes. Pour out your heart to the Lord knowing it is safe. In his book *Ruthless Trust*, Brennan Manning writes, "Raw honesty with Jesus about our doubts and anxieties, our lust and laziness, our shabby prayer life and stale religiosity, our mixed motives and divided hearts is the risk we take in the certainty of being acceptable and accepted."[4]

Worship

You will see that there is a specific place for you to write words of worship to the Lord. You can write single words or a love letter. The form or the quality of your writing doesn't matter because God knows your heart. Just let your thoughts flow. If you love to write and express yourself with many words, you may want to get a separate journal that you can use instead of the small spaces provided. The daily writing is not intended to become a laborious assignment but rather a welcomed time to grow in the Lord and allow him to transform you.

Confession

Next, ask the Lord to reveal any sin you need to confess. If you are uncomfortable writing it down, perhaps you need help addressing it with a safe and mature believer. If you feel it is unsafe to write a particular sin, place an X on the page to represent it and ask God to bring you to complete repentance. I also recommend that you spend time in the book of James, especially chapters 1 and 4. The Word of God is truly living and will work in your spirit as you surrender your will to the Father.

Thankfulness

Thankfulness is the outflow of a contented heart. It is a chosen mind-set and when practiced regularly can cultivate great joy. A person who learns to be thankful for every little blessing—not missing one small gift from God—grows deep roots of contentment that cannot be shaken. Every moment we must choose where we will put our focus—on self or on Christ. That decision will determine the attitude we will cultivate. In his letter to the Colossians, Paul writes, "So then, just as you received Christ Jesus as Lord, continue to live in him, rooted and built up in him, strengthened in the faith as you were taught, and overflowing with thankfulness" (2:6–7). We cannot overflow with thankfulness if we don't take time each day to acknowledge the things for which we are thankful. Ephesians 5:20 says we are to be "always giving thanks to God the Father for everything." Each day, thank God for some of the big and small things in your life.

Prayer Requests

After spending time in worship, confession, and thanksgiving, our prayer requests may be different than if we'd begun with them. Whatever is on your heart and mind, tell God. As it says in Philippians 4:6, "Do not be anxious about anything, but in everything, by prayer and petition, with thanksgiving, present your requests to God." I love that we don't have to submit our list for preapproval. Instead of being anxious about our needs, we can simply talk to God. The next verse does not promise that God will always answer as we desire, but it does give a powerful guarantee: "And the peace of God, which transcends all understanding, will guard your hearts and your minds in Christ Jesus" (v. 7). We don't always understand why God answers our prayers as he does. Sometimes we lack faith. Other times we do not see the whole picture and how an affirmative answer would not produce the best outcome for God's purposes. But we do know that God loves us and has a perfect plan. He may not always give us what we want, but he does always give us what we need. In addition to writing your requests each day, go back once a week and record any answers you have received.

The sample below shows how you can express your thoughts to God in writing. If expressing yourself in writing is difficult, just write single words. This is not an essay test—it is just a place to share your heart with God and a tool to help you review and reflect on what you are learning and what he is teaching you. As you begin this journey, my prayer for you is: Heavenly Father, I pray that you will be glorified as this child of yours pursues you with an open heart. Please pour out your wisdom and grace in ways that encourage a deeper relationship, fully surrendered to you, Lord. Amen.

Example

Worship

Father in heaven, you are the Creator of all things and mighty to be praised. You alone are worthy of my total adoration. I love you and worship you. Great are your works. Great are your plans for those who love you. I stand in awe of you and give you all my praise.

Confession

Lord, I confess I continue to worry and lack faith that you are enough in the midst of life's challenges. I spoke cruel words to my children today and was selfish with my time because I felt so stressed-out. I am still battling with the sin you know all too well and giving in to it rather than fleeing and drawing near to you.

Thankfulness

I am so thankful for my family and friends. They love me despite my poor behavior some days. And of course I'm even more thankful that you have forgiven all my sins—past, present, and future. Thank you for providing jobs in this uncertain time and helping us to be better stewards of our money.

Prayer Requests

Job security and trust in this tough time. Peace for Sally and wisdom for the doctors as they try to diagnose her pain. Please guide our kids in truth and create a hunger in them for you. Keep my eyes on you and help me to recognize your divine appointments.

- From the devotion above I have identified the lie I believe: I believe I am a failure and that God is ashamed of me.
- The truth I now receive: God loves me and wants to give me freedom in Christ. He is on my side. I can go to him despite my behavior because his love is secure.
- I practiced healthy biblical self-talk today (1 to 3 times):
  ☒   ☒   ☒
- My key personal statement is: God loves me just as I am and wants me to run to him in my weakness. When I feel ashamed, I call on his name and he is there.
- I have repeated that message at least three times today:
  ☒   ☒   ☒

- I have written my personal statement above or on an index card so I can continue to read it if I need renewal in this area.
  ☒
- Today I am learning to be more content and joyful by: becoming aware of my attitude and unhealthy self-talk.

Worship

_____

_____

_____

Confession

_____

_____

_____

Thankfulness

_____

_____

_____

Prayer Requests

_____

_____

- From the devotion above I have identified the lie I believe:

  _____

  _____

- The truth I now receive: _____

  _____

  _____

- I practiced healthy biblical self-talk today (1 to 3 times):
  ☐   ☐   ☐

- My key personal statement is:_____

  _____

  _____

- I have repeated that message at least three times today:
  ☐   ☐   ☐

- I have written my personal statement above or on an index card so I can continue to read it if I need renewal in this area.
  ☐

- Today I am learning to be more content and joyful by:

  _____

  _____

Day 1 First Things First

> But seek first his kingdom and his righteousness, and all these things
> will be given to you as well.
>
> Matthew 6:33

First is usually a great place to be. I love being first in line—unless
it's for my mammogram. When I was a little girl, I ran exception-
ally fast and always came in first in our field day competitions. I
even beat the boys! It felt great to be first, with no one ahead of me.
Like most of you, as I got older, first acquired a different meaning.
It became another word for important. In business, I needed to get
the essentials done first. At home, the necessary came first. As a
wife, mother, and employee, my personal needs often came *last*! I'm
guessing you can relate.

Unfortunately, my personal needs included my spiritual life. My
spiritual balloon was often rather deflated. I made excuses. Surely God
understood how early I needed to get up to get the girls ready for school
and get out the door for work. And surely he knew how tired I was by
the time dinner and dishes were done. What should have been first in
my life had become last. What I didn't know was that God wasn't some
spiritual policeman with a checklist of things for me to do each day in
order to be considered worthy. I was already worthy in Christ. When
Jesus told us to "seek first the kingdom of God and his righteousness,"
he was showing us a new lifestyle that would reduce our sense of stress
and striving. The teaching around this Scripture passage is about trusting God to provide for your essential needs—food, clothing, shelter.

In our simplistic thinking, we worry about our needs and make
our first priority "doing." If we live according to God's will, our first
priority should be "being"—being in love with our Creator and giving
our first thoughts and energies to him. He promises that all the things
we really need will be added to our lives. One word of caution: His
definition of need may be different from ours. Romans 14:17 tells
us, "For the kingdom of God is not a matter of eating and drinking,

but of righteousness, peace and joy in the Holy Spirit." Isn't that what we really want and need? Peace and joy?

Fill your spiritual balloon today. Not because you should but because you must. Just as you must eat and drink to live physically, you must eat of God's Word and drink in his goodness each day. We cannot walk by the Spirit or learn to be content in all situations unless we seek God first. He deserves our first thoughts and words. He deserves our first love. He is our first, last, and everything.

Prayer

Father God, forgive me for not putting you first in everything. Please help me to have a burning desire to seek you and your righteousness above all things. Amen.

Worship

_____

_____

_____

Confession

_____

_____

_____

Thankfulness

_____

_____

_____

Prayer Requests

_____

_____

_____

- From the devotion above I have identified the lie I believe:

  _____

  _____

- The truth I now receive: _____

  _____

  _____

- I practiced healthy biblical self-talk today:
  ☐　　☐　　☐

- My key personal statement is:_____

  _____

  _____

- I have repeated that message at least three times today:
  ☐　　☐　　☐

- I have written my personal statement above or on an index card so I can continue to read it if I need renewal in this area.
  ☐

- Today I am learning to be more content and joyful by: _____

  _____

  _____

Day 2 Power in the Vine

I am the vine; you are the branches. If a man remains in me and I in him, he will bear much fruit; apart from me you can do nothing.

John 15:5

The other day my friend and next-door neighbor Curt popped over on a Saturday with his darling ten-month-old Bonnie, just to say hi. Bonnie wants to walk everywhere—she's done with the crawling thing. The only problem is, she can't walk without her Daddy's fingers grasping both of her little hands and giving her continuous balance and security.

In today's verse, Jesus reminds us that we can't "walk" anywhere or accomplish anything of value without his power. "Apart from me you can do nothing"—nothing! It may seem like we are in control, but we are not. I learned that the hard way years ago when my steering wheel actually fell off while I was driving on the freeway. (Obviously I survived. You can read the story in chapter 1). Every breath we take and every move we make happen only by the grace of God.

John 15 describes how we are entwined in an intimate relationship with both Father and Son and that through the power of the

Holy Spirit we can produce fruit (good works that last for eternity) when we stay tightly attached to the vine. Jesus is the vine, the Father is the gardener, and we are the lowly branches. How often have you or I tried to be the vine? It just does not work, because as Jesus says in verse 4, "No branch can bear fruit by itself; it must remain in the vine. Neither can you bear fruit unless you remain in me."

Too many Christians are saved without true victory. They believe that Jesus died for their sins, forgives them, and offers eternal life, but you wouldn't know it to look at their lives. They look and act as miserable as those who are lost—sometimes worse! Sadly, some who profess to know Christ really don't know him at all. A person who is truly indwelt with the Spirit of God desires to bear fruit. Jesus tells us clearly in verse 8, "This is to my Father's glory, that you bear much fruit, showing yourselves to be my disciples."

Prayer

Lord, you alone have the power to produce good fruit in my life. Please show me how and convict me when I am not abiding in you and am trying to do things in my own power. I know you must prune me sometimes, God. Please help me to have the wisdom to know when I am being pruned and to learn from your perfect discipline. Amen.

Worship

_____

_____

_____

Confession

_____

_____

_____

Thankfulness

_____

_____

_____

Prayer Requests

_____

_____

_____

- From the devotion above I have identified the lie I believe:

  _____

  _____

- The truth I now receive: _____

  _____

  _____

- I practiced healthy biblical self-talk today:
  ☐   ☐   ☐

- My key personal statement is:_____

  _____

  _____

- I have repeated that message at least three times today:
  ☐   ☐   ☐

- I have written my personal statement above or on an index card
  so I can continue to read it if I need renewal in this area.
  ☐

- Today I am learning to be more content and joyful by:

  _____

  _____

Day 3 A New Peace

Peace I leave with you; my peace I give you. I do not give to you as
the world gives. Do not let your hearts be troubled and do not be
afraid.

John 14:27

Peace. It means different things to different people. To a mother
of five, all under eight years of age, it means one hour of quiet time
all by herself. To a man who has been struggling to provide for
his family, it means a month free from worrying about bills. To a
frightened wife with an abusive husband, it means he has not lifted
a hand to slap her across the face for a few days. To a family living

in Israel or Palestine, it means a month of living without the sound of air-raid sirens, machine guns, or bombs.

Peace conjures up many images. But the peace Jesus speaks about is beyond our imagination. It is the peace that surpasses all understanding. His peace is all-encompassing. The world's peace is only temporary. The baby wakes up. The man loses his job. The wife gets slapped again. The fighting continues. But the peace of Christ cuts through every situation and gives us the strength and perspective to find contentment—even joy—in the middle of the storm. His peace allows us to look beyond the moment and see the future. "I have told you these things, so that in me you may have peace. In this world you will have trouble. But take heart! I have overcome the world" (John 16:33).

All the pain and fear that threaten our security and shake our foundation are temporary for those who love God. The "rest of the story" is always good for those who know God. In Romans 8:28, Paul writes, "And we know that God causes *all things* to work together for good to those who love God, to those who are called according to His purpose" (NASB, emphasis added).

All things work together for good? Yes, the promise is true for those who love God. But the timing of our realization of the good is not defined. Sometimes God turns something difficult to good in a week. Sometimes we may wait for years. Other times we must wait until heaven. However long the wait, it is the peace of Christ that will sustain us as we set our minds heavenward, realizing that in the bigger scheme of things our wait is very short.

Prayer

Heavenly Father, your peace is what I need. Please help me to keep my mind and heart on you when I am facing the troubles of the world. Help me to trust that you will comfort and sustain me until you work it all together for good. Amen.

Worship

_____

_____

_____

Confession

_____

_____

_____

Thankfulness

_____

_____

_____

Prayer Requests

_____

_____

_____

- From the devotion above I have identified the lie I believe:

_____

_____

- The truth I now receive: _____

  _____

  _____

- I practiced healthy biblical self-talk today:

  ☐   ☐   ☐

- My key personal statement is:_____

  _____

  _____

- I have repeated that message at least three times today:

  ☐   ☐   ☐

- I have written my personal statement above or on an index card so I can continue to read it if I need renewal in this area.

  ☐

- Today I am learning to be more content and joyful by:

  _____

  _____

Day 4 Endless Love

My command is this: Love each other as I have loved you.

John 15:12

The body has a phenomenal way of protecting itself when injured. It sends all its resources to the area of damage to heal and protect it as quickly as possible. In the process, scar tissue is often formed. Those tissues initially meant to protect can often become a problem, inhibiting movement or other important functions. This can also happen to us emotionally, in our soul. When people injure our hearts through betrayal or rejection, we build emotional scar tissue to protect us from future harm. Unfortunately, this type of self-protection diminishes our ability to love fully.

On the unrealistic reality show *The Bachelor*, a rose ceremony closes each episode as the bachelor extends a rose to each woman he wishes to keep on the program and sends one rejected girl away. At the end of the season, two women are left, but only one rose. Both women think they are in love, but one gets rejected in the end—and sent home without a rose.

It occurred to me as I watched a seemingly heartbroken bachelorette sent home without a rose that God has a rose for each of us. He chooses each of us and has more than enough love to fill the holes in our heart completely with authentic, powerful, never-ending love. However, we cannot fully embrace his love and in turn love others until we truly believe on a personal level that his perfect love is real. We must realize that his love is the only love in which we have no risk of being hurt or rejected. Once we accept that truth, the scar tissue on our heart can heal so that we can love others as God intends.

In our key Scripture passage for today, Jesus commands us to love each other as he loved us. He explains the depth of his love in the next verse, which says, "Greater love has no one than this, that one lay down his life for his friends" (John 15:13 NASB).

How many people are you willing to die for? I know most parents would die for their children. And perhaps some spouses would willingly die for each other. Every time one of our United States soldiers goes off to war, he or she is willingly putting his or her life on the line for you and me. Jesus told us to love with this kind of commitment and intentionality. Sacrificial love is so important that he repeated himself again in verse 17: "This is my command: Love each other."

Whether or not you are loved by the people in your life, Jesus loves you completely. He has a rose for you. Its red petals represent the blood he spilled to forgive you of your sins and reconcile you to God for all eternity. Its thorns represent the crown of thorns he wore and the pain he endured on your behalf. When you feel unloved, lonely, or rejected, remember this reality. The power of such love can propel you to love as Jesus commanded—selflessly and with complete abandon.

Prayer

Oh, Lord, your love is overwhelming. Thank you for loving me so much that you sent your only Son to die on my behalf. Please help me to realize your powerful love in a way that fills my heart and causes me to love others as you have loved me. Amen.

Worship

_____

_____

_____

Confession

_____

_____

_____

Thankfulness

_____

_____

_____

Prayer Requests

_____

_____

_____

- From the devotion above I have identified the lie I believe:

  _____

  _____

- The truth I now receive: _____

  _____

  _____

- I practiced healthy biblical self-talk today:
  ☐   ☐   ☐

- My key personal statement is:_____

  _____

  _____

- I have repeated that message at least three times today:
  ☐   ☐   ☐

- I have written my personal statement above or on an index card so I can continue to read it if I need renewal in this area.
☐

- Today I am learning to be more content and joyful by: ____

_____

_____

Day 5 Worthless Worry

Who of you by worrying can add a single hour to his life?

Matthew 6:27

"I have so much to do and so little time to get it done!" Sound familiar? Our days are often filled with an endless list of tasks that leave us "worried and bothered" about so many things (as Jesus said to the type A sister, Martha, in Luke 10). The tyranny of the urgent—or what I call the rubber balls of life—often overwhelms us so that we can't see beyond it.

How often have you stopped in the middle of your busy day and asked, "What difference will all this activity make a year from now?" If and when you do, the answer most likely will be, "No difference at all." Nevertheless, we spend most of our hours working on the things that make very little impact and worrying about things that God is willing to handle.

Jesus tells us in Matthew 6:25–26, "Therefore I tell you, do not worry about your life, what you will eat or drink; or about your body, what you will wear. Is not life more important than food, and the body more important than clothes? Look at the birds of the air; they do not sow or reap or store away in barns, and yet your heavenly Father feeds them. Are you not much more valuable than they?" In other words, we have much more important fish to fry. Our endless activities and lists are not supposed to be our main focus.

What if a sort of cosmic counter tallied up our activities all day long and put them in one of two categories: (1) that which will matter for eternity, and (2) that which will not. How would your scoreboard look at the end of each week? I know mine often looks like my walking in the flesh is beating my walking in the Spirit hands down.

Don't get me wrong. I know the normal activities of life cannot be completely ignored. But when is enough *doing* enough? We cannot hear, let alone follow, the words of Jesus if we are in constant motion. Our stress and worry will not diminish as our efficiency at accomplishing our tasks increases. That is because all those things on our list just return or are replaced with something else day after day.

So what is the answer? How do we transform our worry into peace? We must practice an intentional shift of focus. In the midst of all our doing, we need to lift our eyes to Christ. In the midst of worry, we need to hand our burdens over to him. In the midst of busyness, we need to pray without ceasing and sense his power and peace taking control. We need to let go of what we cannot control and cannot accomplish and spend more moments investing in what will last forever.

Prayer

Lord God, I need to learn how to stop being such an excellent human "doing" and sit at your feet and transform into a human being. Please give me the wisdom to choose the best from all the good in my day. Please help me to let go of worry and instead look to you for the peace that surpasses all understanding. Thank you, Lord.

Worship

_____

_____

_____

Confession

_____

_____

_____

Thankfulness

_____

_____

_____

Prayer Requests

_____

_____

_____

- From the devotion above I have identified the lie I believe:

_____

_____

- The truth I now receive: _____

  _____

  _____

- I practiced healthy biblical self-talk today:
  ☐   ☐   ☐

- My key personal statement is:_____

  _____

  _____

- I have repeated that message at least three times today:
  ☐   ☐   ☐

- I have written my personal statement above or on an index card so I can continue to read it if I need renewal in this area.
  ☐

- Today I am learning to be more content and joyful by:

  _____

  _____

Day 6 The Overflow of Praise

For out of the overflow of the heart the mouth speaks.

Matthew 12:34

I'm so mad. I'm so happy. I love my life. I hate my life. You are so kind. God is so good. I'm afraid. I can't do this. God will help me. I feel so alone. God is always with me. I can't take this anymore. The Lord is my strength. What words flow from your heart and mouth most days?

Our verse for today reminds me of a story about a spry ninety-two-year-old woman. She dressed each morning by eight o'clock, with her hair fashionably done and makeup perfectly applied, even though she was legally blind. Her husband of seventy years had recently passed away, and she needed to move to a nursing home for some assistance.

The day of the move, she spent many hours waiting patiently in the lobby of her new residence. She smiled sweetly when told her room was ready and listened intently as the employee provided a visual description of her tiny room. "I love it," she stated with enthusiasm.

The employee replied, "Mrs. Jones, you haven't seen the room. Just wait."

"That doesn't have anything to do with it," she answered. "Happiness is something you decide on ahead of time. Whether I like my room or not doesn't depend on how the furniture is arranged. It's how I arrange my mind. I already decided to love it. It's a decision I make every morning when I wake up. I have a choice; I can spend the day in bed recounting the difficulty I have with the parts of my body that no longer work, or I can get out of bed and be thankful for the ones that do."

Our words betray our heart. We may try to hold our tongue at times and not speak our mind. But if we listen carefully, our words (both silent and spoken) express what we have hidden there. What are your words saying about the condition of your heart? If you have identified some of the lies you believe and have decided to replace those lies with God's truth, your heart and mind will eventually change . . . and so will the words that flow from your mouth.

Prayer

Father God, please help me to deposit your truth and hope into my heart each day by spending more time in your Word and prayer.

Where I have doubts and fear, please increase my faith. Where I have discontentment, please fill my heart with gratitude. Amen.

Worship

_____

_____

_____

Confession

_____

_____

_____

Thankfulness

_____

_____

_____

Prayer Requests

_____

_____

_____

- From the devotion above I have identified the lie I believe:

  _____

  _____

- The truth I now receive: _____

  _____

  _____

- I practiced healthy biblical self-talk today:
  ☐   ☐   ☐

- My key personal statement is:_____

  _____

  _____

- I have repeated that message at least three times today:
  ☐   ☐   ☐

- I have written my personal statement above or on an index card so I can continue to read it if I need renewal in this area.
  ☐

- Today I am learning to be more content and joyful by:

  _____

  _____

Day 7 Run Home

> But while he was still a long way off, his father saw him and was filled
> with compassion for him; he ran to his son, threw his arms around
> him and kissed him.
>
> Luke 15:20

Have you ever spent hours anxiously worrying about a teenager
who never bothered to call to say she would be late? You run the
gamut of emotions from fear to anger. What if that child left in a
selfish and destructive way and stayed away a long, long time? In a
difficult season of my life, my young adult daughters were gone for
many months. Sometimes I agonized about their well-being and
wondered if they were hurt or dead. I hoped my girls did not fear
coming home and waited prayerfully for that day.

In what many call the parable of the prodigal son, Jesus tells the
story of a younger son who wanted his share of his father's wealth
immediately. The son represents all of us who want to have it our own
way. The father (representing God) grants his son's request, and with
his money in hand, the son leaves the family, only to squander his
money in short order. Far from home, he must resort to becoming
a hired hand and eating with the pigs. He is miserable and alone.
Coming to his senses and realizing the error of his choices, he desires
to go home and executes a plan. In Luke 15:18, he says, "I will set
out and go back to my father and say to him: Father, I have sinned
against heaven and against you. I am no longer worthy to be called
your son; make me like one of your hired men."

How would you respond if your son or daughter had wasted
everything you had given them? What would your initial reaction
be as they turned the bend toward home? The prodigal son was
ready for the worst, willing to become his father's slave. But nothing could have prepared him for what he received—his father's
passionate welcome and loving embrace. Not only did his father
receive him with open arms, but he also prepared a feast and put

his best robe across his shoulders, a ring on his hand, and sandals on his feet.

Our Father in heaven opens his arms to us when we return to him with a repentant heart. Like the lost son, we need to change our mind, surrender our heart, and turn away from our previous sin. The father could have rejected the son. He could have made him jump through hoops and prove his worthiness to receive forgiveness and mercy. But he didn't. Our perfect Father knows that we need mercy and grace in order to move forward. Otherwise, we become paralyzed in our guilt and shame.

It is never too late to go home to your loving and merciful God. He knows everything about you and loves you anyway. He wants all of you and waits expectantly for you to realize that he is all you really need. If you've been running, isn't it time to finally run home . . . straight into the arms of God?

Prayer

Heavenly Father, holy God, it is amazing and comforting to know that you love me despite my behavior. You know the places in my life where I have been running from you. I need to turn away from them and run to you. Please forgive me for trying to do life my way. Help me to fully embrace that your ways are best and that I will find true and lasting satisfaction only by following them. Amen.

Worship

_____

_____

_____

Confession

_____

_____

_____

Thankfulness

_____

_____

_____

Prayer Requests

_____

_____

_____

- From the devotion above I have identified the lie I believe:

  _____

  _____

- The truth I now receive: _____

  _____

  _____

- I practiced healthy biblical self-talk today:
  ☐   ☐   ☐

- My key personal statement is:_____

  _____

  _____

- I have repeated that message at least three times today:

  ☐   ☐   ☐

- I have written my personal statement above or on an index card so I can continue to read it if I need renewal in this area.

  ☐

- Today I am learning to be more content and joyful by: _____

  _____

  _____

Day 8 Faith without Doubt

Then Jesus told him, "Because you have seen me, you have believed; blessed are those who have not seen and yet have believed."

John 20:29

Have you ever used the phrase "you're a doubting Thomas"? My pastor, Tim Scott, gave me a new perspective on Thomas's apparent lack of faith. In truth, don't we all want to substantiate our faith? Perhaps Thomas simply wanted to experience what the other disciples had: a personal glimpse of Jesus in his resurrected body. They had all excitedly reported their experience to him. Since they were his close friends and spiritual brothers, it is unlikely he doubted their words. More likely, he passionately desired to experience the resurrected Lord for himself, and so he said to them, "Unless I see the nail marks in his hands and put my finger where the nails were, and put my hand into his side, I will not believe it" (John 20:25).

Thomas declared that he wanted to see the facts. It was a valid request. And it is interesting to note that to be considered an apostle and for one's teaching and writing to be accepted, that person had to have seen and walked with the resurrected Lord. It *was* reasonable for Thomas to seek visible evidence. Christ responded directly to his request, giving him full opportunity to see, touch, and feel the evidence of his resurrection in a personal and intimate way: "Then he said to Thomas, 'Put your finger here; see my hands. Reach out your hand and put it into my side. Stop doubting and believe'" (John 20:27). Jesus's words had incredible substance and power, and Thomas exclaimed, "My Lord and my God!" (John 20:28).

We will not have the same opportunity to see Christ in his resurrected body until he returns again. However, we do not need to ask for empirical evidence because we have substantiated historical facts based on many credible eyewitnesses, such as Thomas.

Jesus said to Thomas, "Because you have seen me, you have believed; blessed are those who have not seen and yet have believed" (John 20:29). We are the ones Jesus was speaking of who would need to believe based on the account of so many others. Faith is not blind. Faith is not a leap in the dark. As it says in Hebrews 11:1, "Now faith is being sure of what we hope for and certain of what we do not see." We can be sure. We are certain. Even though we have not seen Christ yet, we will . . . and our joy will be made complete.

Prayer

Father in heaven, praise your holy name! Thank you for giving us an account of those who witnessed Christ in his resurrected body so we can believe with certainty that our faith is real. Thank you for calling us blessed for believing without seeing. I look forward to seeing you one day and touching you as Thomas did. Until then, I believe in faith that you are the risen Lord! Amen.

Worship

_____

_____

_____

Confession

_____

_____

_____

Thankfulness

_____

_____

_____

Prayer Requests

_____

_____

_____

- From the devotion above I have identified the lie I believe:

  _____

  _____

- The truth I now receive: _____

  _____

  _____

- I practiced healthy biblical self-talk today:
  ☐   ☐   ☐

- My key personal statement is:_____

  _____

  _____

- I have repeated that message at least three times today:
  ☐   ☐   ☐

- I have written my personal statement above or on an index card
  so I can continue to read it if I need renewal in this area.
  ☐

- Today I am learning to be more content and joyful by: ____

  _____

  _____

Day 9 One Way

Jesus answered, "I am the way and the truth and the life. No one comes to the Father except through me."

John 14:6

Finding a parking place in a full lot can be so frustrating. It was raining the day I'm thinking about, and I was late getting to an event my grown daughter had invited me to attend. Then I noticed one more row of cars with a space available at the very end. I could see that the arrow on the asphalt was pointing at me, indicating I would be going the wrong way if I drove directly to the spot I coveted. But if I didn't, I would have to leave the parking lot, go back onto the street, and find another way in to get to the spot, which would surely be gone by the time I got there.

I believe in rules. I know they are designed for a purpose, but I saw no harm in going the wrong direction just this once. No one was coming toward me, and I was not being unsafe. I was late for goodness sake! Well, the police officer hidden at the very end of the parking lot did not agree with my reasoning and gruffly admonished, "One way means one way, Miss." He proceeded to write me a ticket, and I ended up going to traffic school to keep my impeccable record clean. I also paid a hefty fine for my "moving violation." Is going five miles an hour really considered moving?

Jesus said, "I am the way and the truth and the life. No one comes to the Father except through me" (John 14:6). He makes it pretty clear. We can try a shortcut—but it won't get us to heaven. We can hope and pray that God didn't really mean what he said—but he does. In Acts 4:12, Peter says to the rulers and leaders of the day who were responsible for crucifying Jesus, "Salvation is found in no one else, for there is no other name under heaven given to men by which we must be saved."

I've talked to people who say things like, "My God would not be so close minded and cruel to allow good people to go to hell just because they don't believe in Jesus." I want to say, "Your God does not exist." After Jesus said that he was the only way to God, he continued in verse 7, saying, "If you really knew me, you would know my Father as well. From now on, you do know him and have seen him." In verse 11, he further clarifies that he and the Father are one: "Believe me when I say that I am in the Father and the Father is in me; or at least believe on the evidence of the miracles themselves."

God gave Adam and Eve everything they could possibly want or need to live a perfect life. He also gave them a free will and one simple rule: Don't eat of the tree of the knowledge of good and evil. They ate, and man fell from grace with God. As a result, we all became contaminated with sin and sentenced to death. God had no obligation to provide a way out of our condemnation. But "God so loved the world that he gave his one and only Son" (John 3:16). What an incredibly loving, merciful sacrifice. Some say the way to heaven is too narrow, but I say, "Thank you, Lord, for providing such a beautiful crimson path to eternal life."

When we are feeling like life is less than we'd hoped or more painful than we'd expected, let us remember Jesus's pain and sacrifice. Let us remember that this life is not the ultimate one. It is just a blip in time. And not only is Jesus the only way to the Father and heaven, he is also the only way to find peace and contentment today.

Living in the Italian part of Switzerland for two years and attending church there, I heard the verse above many times in that language. It reads like this: "Io sono la via, la verita, i la vita." In any and every language, the hope of eternity reads the same: Jesus . . . Jesus . . . Jesus!

Prayer

Heavenly Father, thank you for the way, the truth, and the life, which are found only in Jesus. Please help me to more fully understand your sacrifice. Give me the words to share your hope of salvation with those who are lost. Amen.

Worship

_____

_____

_____

Confession

_____

_____

_____

Thankfulness

_____

_____

_____

Prayer Requests

_____

_____

_____

- From the devotion above I have identified the lie I believe:

  _____

  _____

- The truth I now receive: _____

  _____

  _____

- I practiced healthy biblical self-talk today:
  ☐   ☐   ☐

- My key personal statement is:_____

  _____

  _____

- I have repeated that message at least three times today:
  ☐   ☐   ☐

- I have written my personal statement above or on an index card
  so I can continue to read it if I need renewal in this area.
  ☐

- Today I am learning to be more content and joyful by: _____

  _____

  _____

Day 10 In Jesus's Name

And I will do whatever you ask in my name, so that the Son may bring glory to the Father. You may ask me for anything in my name, and I will do it.

John 14:13–14

As they entered the candy shop, the young mother said to her son, "You can have anything you want, honey."

"*Anything?*" he replied incredulously in his squeaky six-year-old voice. Of course the mother did not mean he could have *everything* in the store. And she had limits on when and how much the boy could eat. Like the child who needed full understanding before he raided the entire candy store, we must understand what Jesus means when he says that we can ask for *anything* in his name and he will do it.

Bible scholar and Christian radio host Greg Koukl says this about using the authority of someone's name:

> The name of someone, in the sense that the Bible authors used it, was what the person stood for, the substance of their character, or their authority. When we pray in the name of Jesus or baptize in the name of the Father, Son, and Holy Spirit, what we are doing is acting in their authority, in their stead, according to their command, and *consistent with their desires*. There is power in praying in the authority of Jesus Christ, by the authority He has given you, consistent with His character, His desire, and His will. It's like when we say, "Stop in the name of the law." The policeman is saying that because he is standing in the place of the law and speaking on behalf of it. To the degree that he speaks for the law, then he can enforce the law and he has authority. When he steps outside of the law, he has lost his authority even though he still says, "Stop in the name of the law."[1]

Jesus is very clear in the verse above that his purpose is to bring glory to the Father. If we ask him for something by the authority of his name that will indeed bring glory to God, we can be sure he will do it. Sadly, we've used "in Jesus's name" as a rote end to almost every prayer. Does ending my petitions in this way somehow obligate God to answer? Of course not. And, in fact, I've become convicted that like the Pharisees I am in one sense praying with vain repetitions.

Prayer is a powerful privilege, yet it never obligates God to respond according to our will. We should know God's Word so thoroughly that we rarely pray outside his perfect will. In Romans 12:2, we are told, "Do not conform any longer to the pattern of this world, but be transformed by the renewing of your mind. Then you will be able to test and approve what God's will is—his good, pleasing and perfect will." Our minds are renewed by God's truth. His Word is living and active. When it permeates our mind, we cannot help but know God's will and ask in accordance with it.

Prayer

Father in heaven, I want to know and do your will. Please give me an unquenchable thirst for your Word that drives me to the Bible every day. Renew my mind so I can test and approve what is worthy to ask in your name. Amen.

Worship

_____

_____

_____

Confession

_____

_____

_____

Thankfulness

_____

_____

_____

Prayer Requests

_____

_____

_____

- From the devotion above I have identified the lie I believe:

  _____

  _____

- The truth I now receive: _____

  _____

  _____

- I practiced healthy biblical self-talk today:
  ☐   ☐   ☐

- My key personal statement is:_____

  _____

  _____

- I have repeated that message at least three times today:
  ☐   ☐   ☐

- I have written my personal statement above or on an index card
  so I can continue to read it if I need renewal in this area.
  ☐

- Today I am learning to be more content and joyful by: _____

  _____

  _____

Day 11 Selfless Serving

> Now that I, your Lord and Teacher, have washed your feet, you also
> should wash one another's feet.
>
> John 13:14

Have you ever felt hurt when everyone else in your group got to do something meaningful and you were assigned a meager job that had little importance? Or perhaps you watch other people in a role you'd like to have and think, "Not fair. I could do that so much better!" Our perception of value can be skewed if we look at our roles in the context of the world's values. In our culture, those who serve others are generally looked upon as less important than those who do almost anything else. If you work (or have ever worked) in a service job, people may treat you poorly. Even worse, others may act as if you don't even exist.

Imagine for a moment someone you greatly respect serving you in the most humble of ways. What if the president of the United States came to your home and acted as your butler for a week? Or your pastor became your chauffeur for a month? What would you think if the surgeon who did your husband's bypass surgery asked if he could clean your house and take out the garbage? These are all seemingly absurd images. If they actually happened, we would be shocked and probably quite uncomfortable. Someone we hold in high esteem serving us in such a lowly way is hard to accept. That is exactly what Jesus did.

In his day, people walked everywhere. Their feet got hot, tired, and dirty. The household servants were relegated to the task of washing their master's and his guests' feet. Yet, on this day Jesus washed his disciples' feet and told them to do the same for each other. He left them with a powerful picture of what it means to serve despite your position. Jesus needed to make sure they understood what was truly important to him—love and serving out of love. He had told them that the last would be first and the first would be last (Mark 10:31). He had also told them to love each other as he had loved them. Now, he showed them what that looked like. It was a beautiful expression of humility and submission. That is how Jesus came to the earth. He lowered himself to give his perfect life so we could be forgiven by his blood and live forever in his presence.

Serving is a beautiful expression of humility. No matter how people treat us when we serve, we know we are honoring the Lord and reflecting his example.

Prayer

Father, thank you for showing us the beauty of humility in Jesus. Please help me to have a humble servant's heart no matter how others may see or treat me. I love you and want to serve you above all. Amen.

Worship

_____

_____

_____

Confession

_____

_____

_____

Thankfulness

_____

_____

_____

Prayer Requests

_____

_____

_____

- From the devotion above I have identified the lie I believe:

  _____

  _____

- The truth I now receive: _____

  _____

  _____

- I practiced healthy biblical self-talk today:

  ☐   ☐   ☐

- My key personal statement is:_____

  _____

  _____

- I have repeated that message at least three times today:

  ☐   ☐   ☐

- I have written my personal statement above or on an index card so I can continue to read it if I need renewal in this area.

  ☐

- Today I am learning to be more content and joyful by: _____

  _____

  _____

Day 12 Second Chances

"I tell you the truth," Jesus answered, "today—yes, tonight—before
the rooster crows twice you yourself will disown me three times."

Mark 14:30

In my walk with Christ over the last thirty-five years, I've had some
pretty significant ups and downs. There have been times when I felt like
he had taken me to the top of the mountain, where I could see more
clearly than ever before. I have been overwhelmed with the power of
his love in my life. I can remember telling him that I would always stay
close and would never let *anything* get in the way of my relationship
with him ever again. In those moments, I sensed such an incredible,
deep connection with God through Christ that I could not imagine
ever feeling any differently. Somehow as the months and years flew by,
the ebbs and flows of life distracted me, and my commitment to the
Lord weakened in tiny increments. One day I realized I had walked
so far away that he was no longer the center of my life.

When Peter told Jesus, "Even if I have to die with you, I will never
disown you" (Matt. 26:35) with all the passion and commitment he
felt in his soul, Jesus responded with the words, "Before the rooster
crows twice you yourself will disown me three times." His reply
must have stung Peter's heart. How could Jesus say such a thing
when Peter loved him so completely? Jesus knows our weaknesses.
We get scared . . . distracted . . . confused . . . self-absorbed. And
despite our good intentions, we take Jesus off his rightful throne.

Imagine being Peter for a moment. Just hours after that passionate
promise, the Lord is wrenched away by hostile soldiers, and you are
frightened about what this may mean for you. So words slip out of
your mouth in self-protection. "I don't know the man!" (Matt. 26:72).
You deny knowing him three times, and then the rooster crows and
you remember what Jesus said. Peter's response: "He broke down
and wept" (Mark 14:72).

We are so weak. Even when our intentions are good, we often
fail. We desperately need the forgiveness and strength of a Savior.

He is so good, loving, and perfect. Fortunately, the story did not end when the rooster crowed. The resurrected Savior met Peter on the beach and asked him three times if he loved him. Peter needed to respond three times, not to convince Jesus but to convince himself. Each time Peter answered, "You know that I love you," Jesus commissioned him to live out his faith by giving him a command. Jesus responded first, "Feed my lambs." The second time, "Take care of my sheep." And the last time, "Feed my sheep!" (John 21:15–17). Peter now was commissioned to demonstrate his love for Christ by pouring his life into others. Sheep are weak. They need shepherding. We all do.

Despite our best intentions, we can walk consistently with Christ in the details of life only when we continually surrender every corner of our life to him. And even then, the flesh is weak. But the Savior is full of mercy and grace. He has a plan and purpose for our lives. Do you love him? Then demonstrate your love by dedicating your life to his service. It is the only thing that will bring you total fulfillment and complete joy.

Prayer

Heavenly Father, thank you for your incredible forgiveness, mercy, and grace. I want to follow you with all my heart. That is my intention, but I cannot do it without your supernatural power. Help me to dedicate each new day to you . . . each new moment. Amen.

Worship

_____

_____

_____

Confession

_____

_____

_____

Thankfulness

_____

_____

_____

Prayer Requests

_____

_____

_____

- From the devotion above I have identified the lie I believe:

  _____

  _____

- The truth I now receive: _____

  _____

  _____

- I practiced healthy biblical self-talk today:
  ☐   ☐   ☐

- My key personal statement is:_____

  _____

  _____

- I have repeated that message at least three times today:
  ☐   ☐   ☐

- I have written my personal statement above or on an index card
  so I can continue to read it if I need renewal in this area.
  ☐

- Today I am learning to be more content and joyful by: _____

  _____

  _____

Day 13 Exclusive Worship

Jesus answered, "It is written: 'Worship the Lord your God and serve him only.'"

Luke 4:8

The crowd went crazy when the quarterback scored the winning touchdown in the last minutes of the game. Everyone was jumping up and down, screaming the hero's name, and celebrating the victory. The scene a few weeks later at the Super Bowl was even more intense when the team pulled out all the stops and grabbed hold of the ultimate prize. The entire city was buzzing with energy. People could not stop talking about the game, the team, the talented quarterback.

Football heroes, singing stars, and famous actors seem to mesmerize us with their success and lifestyles. We are bombarded with magazines flaunting their latest activity and television shows telling us everything we would ever want to know about them. Many Americans worship the idea of celebrity, and some attempt to live vicariously through the people who seem to have it all.

When we lived in Lugano, Switzerland, we were only minutes away from Lake Como, Italy. People asked me all the time if I had seen George Clooney. I had no idea that almost everyone knew he had a villa there. I found the question rather funny. Nobody asked me if I'd seen the pope when I went to Rome! After a year of being asked the same question dozens of times, I sent out an email to a large group of women with the following subject line: GC sighting.

Yep, not only did I *see* George but I sat about twenty feet away from him for an entire three-hour dinner! In the body of my email, I told a funny story about him putting a spoon on his nose and smiling at me. Imagine that—I was *spooned* by George Clooney! Then in closing, I said what was really on my heart: "While it was fun to finally be able to answer, 'Yes, yes, I've seen George' to all the questions, quite honestly, I truly wish I could have had a JC sighting instead!"

One day, those of us who know Jesus as our Savior and Lord will actually see him coming in the clouds in power and glory (Mark 13:26). And he'll be coming for us! Until that day, we must be careful to guard our hearts and minds. It's so easy to get infatuated with the accomplishments of others. Even Christians have a tendency to be attracted to celebrity and put certain people up on pedestals. While they may have earned our respect, they are still merely human. Jesus tells us to worship the Lord our God and to serve him only. Sadly, we are all guilty of worshiping many things and people rather than the one who deserves our worship and praise.

Prayer

Holy, perfect God, you alone are worthy of our worship. Please show me when I am becoming infatuated with people to the extent that I almost worship what they represent. Show me when work, goals, and even ministry compete with my love for you. I want to worship you and you only. Amen.

Worship

_____

_____

_____

Confession

_____

_____

_____

Thankfulness

_____

_____

_____

Prayer Requests

_____

_____

_____

- From the devotion above I have identified the lie I believe:

  _____

  _____

- The truth I now receive: _____

  _____

  _____

- I practiced healthy biblical self-talk today:
  ☐   ☐   ☐

- My key personal statement is:_____

  _____

  _____

- I have repeated that message at least three times today:
  ☐   ☐   ☐

- I have written my personal statement above or on an index card so I can continue to read it if I need renewal in this area.
  ☐

- Today I am learning to be more content and joyful by: _____

_____

_____

Day 14 God Provides

"Here is a boy with five small barley loaves and two small fish, but how far will they go among so many?" . . . Jesus then took the loaves, gave thanks, and distributed to those who were seated as much as they wanted. He did the same with the fish. When they had all had enough to eat, he said to his disciples, "Gather the pieces that are left over. Let nothing be wasted." So they gathered them and filled twelve baskets with the pieces of the five barley loaves left over by those who had eaten.

John 6:9, 11–13

Have you ever imagined sitting on the grass with five thousand other people and personally witnessing the miracle of Jesus feeding such a multitude? There was enough for all to eat, and still food was left over. Absolutely amazing!

The Bible tells us, "Jesus Christ is the same yesterday and today and forever" (Heb. 13:8). He is able to satisfy our needs each day. When we are at the end of ourselves and have done all that is humanly possible, he provides—sometimes for the day and sometimes above and beyond what we could ask or imagine. In this case, Scripture tells us it would have taken eight months' wages to give each person in the crowd just one bite of bread; yet they all ate until they were full.

You read Kimberly's story about being abandoned with five children in a broken-down home with no significant income. One month, when finances were depleted and the mortgage was due, she had to choose between groceries or making the house payment. In desperation, she prayed to the Lord to provide a miracle for her family. The next day her son ran into the house holding a white-gold and diamond watch he had found in the ivy in the front yard. He gave it to her, and she was stunned by the price tag still attached. The watch was priced at over fifteen hundred dollars! Later that day she took it to a reputable jeweler who offered the very amount needed to make the mortgage payment. That day she knew that God would always be faithful to care for her family. Jesus is the same yesterday, today, and forever, and he provides for his children.

Often I have quoted Oswald Chambers, who said, "We are in danger of forgetting that we cannot do what God does, and that God will not do what we can do."[1] Elbert Hubbard says something similar in a much-less spiritual (and a lot more humorous) way. "Parties who want milk should not seat themselves on a stool in the middle of the field in hopes that the cow will back up to them."[2] Many times in God's Word we are told to trust him to provide for our daily needs. But we are also told not to be sluggards—a name that speaks for itself. We must balance the promises of God with his teaching about responsibility and work. Sometimes we also mix up the difference between need and want. I've been guilty of calling out to God to help me cover bills that I had no business accumulating in the first place. And in those times when need and greed got confused, he disciplined me as a loved child who needed to learn how to live by all his precepts, not just the ones I liked!

Prayer

Heavenly Father, thank you for taking care of our daily needs—sometimes even miraculously. Help me to know the difference between need and want. Help me to understand why your answer is sometimes no when I have not been obedient in following your ways. Amen.

Worship

_____

_____

_____

Confession

_____

_____

_____

Thankfulness

_____

_____

_____

Prayer Requests

_____

_____

_____

- From the devotion above I have identified the lie I believe:

_____

_____

- The truth I now receive: _____

  _____

  _____

- I practiced healthy biblical self-talk today:
  ☐　　☐　　☐

- My key personal statement is:_____

  _____

  _____

- I have repeated that message at least three times today:
  ☐　　☐　　☐

- I have written my personal statement above or on an index card so I can continue to read it if I need renewal in this area.
  ☐

- Today I am learning to be more content and joyful by: ____

  _____

  _____

Day 15 Divinely Led

All this I have spoken while still with you. But the Counselor, the Holy Spirit, whom the Father will send in my name, will teach you all things and will remind you of everything I have said to you.

John 14:25–26

My husband has been a fantastic role model and personal coach to our son, Jesse, who is almost thirteen and in the seventh grade. Lew (who has a military and strong leadership background) is always saying things to Jesse such as, "Be a leader!" and "Leaders always lead!" Recently, Jesse began playing tackle football for the very first time, and when Lew asked him if he was being a leader on his team, Jesse replied with great wisdom, saying, "Dad, I'm just learning how to play football. Before I'm a leader, I need to be led."

We all need to be led . . . all the time . . . by the Holy Spirit of the living God! If we ever come to the place that we think we have studied the Bible and walked with God so long that we have all the answers, we are wrong. We can become leaders in ministry and the church, but our effectiveness will be dependent on our sensitivity to the continual leading of the Holy Spirit. He is always with us, leading and convicting us.

Jesus told the disciples that even though he was leaving them physically, they would never be alone again. He called the Holy Spirit the Counselor. How wonderful that all the wisdom of the universe is available to us all the time. If we fill our mind with God's Word, the Holy Spirit will continually remind us of it and help us not only understand it but also apply it to our lives. He guides us in all truth.

If you are unsure whether the Spirit is leading you or you are simply responding to your own wishes and desires, go to the Word of God. The Spirit will never lead you in contradiction to the Word. If you are unsure, don't take action. I have found in my own life that feeling peace can often be a deception, and I am simply rationalizing what I want. We say things like, "I feel peace about buying this new home." Or, "I feel peace about this relationship." I've felt peace about a lot of things that ended up being bad decisions. If it meant buying something I could not afford, I was probably feeling my own desire rather than sensing the prompting of the Holy Spirit. We can become dulled to the Counselor's leading and even grieve him (Eph. 4:29–31) if we are not fully surrendered to making Christ Lord of our lives and responding to the truth we have been given. The Spirit is always ready and willing to teach us and remind us of God's way, but we must be willing to open our hearts and minds to his leading!

Prayer

God in heaven, thank you for sealing me with your Holy Spirit—who lives in me and will teach and guide me. Please help me not to grieve him and to submit to his leading. Amen.

Worship

_____

_____

_____

Confession

_____

_____

_____

Thankfulness

_____

_____

_____

Prayer Requests

_____

_____

_____

- From the devotion above I have identified the lie I believe:

  _____

  _____

- The truth I now receive: _____

  _____

  _____

- I practiced healthy biblical self-talk today:
  ☐   ☐   ☐

- My key personal statement is:_____

  _____

  _____

- I have repeated that message at least three times today:
  ☐   ☐   ☐

- I have written my personal statement above or on an index card so I can continue to read it if I need renewal in this area.
  ☐

- Today I am learning to be more content and joyful by: ____

_____

_____

Day 16 Loving Discipline

Those whom I love I rebuke and discipline. So be earnest, and repent. Here I am! I stand at the door and knock. If anyone hears my voice and opens the door, I will come in and eat with him, and he with me.

Revelation 3:19–20

Discipline. Isn't that something children eighteen and younger must endure to become mature adults? Sometimes it seems as though our children don't understand the concept of unacceptable behavior. As parents, our job is to explain our expectations and guide them with discipline so they can grow in character. As we set healthy boundaries, they feel safe and loved.

My son, Jesse, has a type A personality (like me) and a tendency to speak his mind in a disrespectful way at times. In years past when my husband overheard him being ill-mannered to me, he would say, "Apologize to your mother before you take your time-out." It was obvious to me that a muttered "Sorry, Mom" meant almost nothing. Instead of an apology, I began asking Jesse to respond to an important question: "What was wrong with what just happened?" Amazingly, this question required him to think about his actions and consider what he had said or done wrong.

Over time, he became more insightful, and I could hear the remorse in his voice when he described his wrongdoing. One day, I had to hold back my laughter when he said in a grave little-boy voice, "Mom, I don't think I'm going to live very long."

"Why's that, Jesse?" I asked with all the seriousness I could muster.

He replied with a trembling voice, "Because I don't honor you and Dad like I should, and the Bible says I need to do that to have a long life." We had the most amazing hug and then talked about the grace of God and forgiveness.

Jesus disciplines us because he loves us. He wants us to understand the importance of our thoughts, words, and actions. Empty apologies mean nothing—but earnest repentance is a wonderful step toward restored relationship. Jesus is always ready to spend intimate time with us. As we walk through the challenges of our lives, we don't always know if the Lord is disciplining us. But we do know that he does not waste our experiences. I know he will give you insight if you ask him, "Lord, what would you have me learn from this situation?" When our lives are surrendered and we consistently repent of our sins, he stands at the door and knocks—desiring intimacy and connection.

Prayer

Dear Lord, thank you for loving me enough to discipline me and show me a better way. Please give me the wisdom to understand your Word so that I may follow you more closely. Thank you for always being available to have a deep relationship with me. I love you. Amen.

Worship

_____

_____

_____

Confession

_____

_____

_____

Thankfulness

_____

_____

_____

Prayer Requests

_____

_____

_____

- From the devotion above I have identified the lie I believe:

  _____

  _____

- The truth I now receive: _____

  _____

  _____

- I practiced healthy biblical self-talk today:
  ☐   ☐   ☐

- My key personal statement is:_____

  _____

  _____

- I have repeated that message at least three times today:

  ☐   ☐   ☐

- I have written my personal statement above or on an index card

  so I can continue to read it if I need renewal in this area.

  ☐

- Today I am learning to be more content and joyful by: _____

  _____

  _____

Day 17 Me . . . Humble?

For whoever exalts himself will be humbled, and whoever humbles
himself will be exalted.

Matthew 23:12

You can't help but laugh at the words of a country song by Mac Davis:
"Oh, Lord, it's hard to be humble when I'm perfect in every way." Few
of us feel that way very often. And when we do, if we're honest, it actually feels really good. When we finish an important task and do a great
job, we have a wonderful sense of accomplishment. If we get some new
clothes and a new haircut and look our very best and people notice,
that feels great too! But that's not what Jesus is speaking about here. He
is warning us not to think of ourselves as more important than others
but rather to consider others more important than ourselves. As it says

in Philippians 2:3, "Do nothing out of selfish ambition or vain conceit, but in humility consider others better than yourselves."

Webster's Dictionary defines humility as "not proud or haughty; not arrogant or assertive; offered in a spirit of deference or submission; insignificant; unpretentious." The Bible contains seventy-one references with the word *humble* and more when you search for other tenses of the word. Humility is important to God. Christ modeled it in every way despite his deity—despite his power. Philippians 2:5–8 says, "Your attitude should be the same as that of Christ Jesus: Who, being in very nature God, did not consider equality with God something to be grasped, but made himself nothing, taking the very nature of a servant, being made in human likeness. And being found in appearance as a man, he humbled himself and became obedient to death—even death on a cross!"

In this day and age, parents are continually told to build their children's self-confidence so they can become successful in life. In reality, the techniques used to build such self-esteem also promote selfishness and self-absorption. Notice the recurring theme of self . . . self . . . self. In contrast, as believers we realize we need more of Christ and less of self. We need to find our identity, security, and gratification through growing in *Christ*-confidence. This kind of godly confidence reminds us that everything we say or do that has any value is only by the power and grace of God. It gives us a selfless and grateful perspective that keeps us from thinking more highly of ourselves than we should. And in the end, God has a wonderful reward for a life lived in humility and submission: "Humble yourselves, therefore, under God's mighty hand, that he may lift you up in due time. Cast all your anxiety on him because he cares for you" (1 Peter 5:6–7).

Prayer

Heavenly Father, please show me when I am self-centered and self-promoting. Help me to be acutely aware that everything good in me is only because of you. May my confidence be in Christ alone. Amen.

Worship

_____

_____

_____

Confession

_____

_____

_____

Thankfulness

_____

_____

_____

Prayer Requests

_____

_____

_____

- From the devotion above I have identified the lie I believe:

  _____

  _____

- The truth I now receive: _____

  _____

  _____

- I practiced healthy biblical self-talk today:
  ☐   ☐   ☐

- My key personal statement is:_____

  _____

  _____

- I have repeated that message at least three times today:
  ☐   ☐   ☐

- I have written my personal statement above or on an index card
  so I can continue to read it if I need renewal in this area.
  ☐

- Today I am learning to be more content and joyful by: _____

  _____

  _____

Day 18 Flavorful Living

You are the salt of the earth. But if the salt loses its saltiness, how can it be made salty again? It is no longer good for anything, except to be thrown out and trampled by men.

Matthew 5:13

Salt. I just love it. It brings out the flavor of food in a magical way. But without it, the most delectable-looking treat can taste like Styrofoam. Since I don't eat a lot of pastries and sweets, when I do have something, I want it to be worth the extra calories. So you can imagine my disappointment when I chose to indulge in new and special delicacies while living in Europe only to find them tasteless. Time after time, I'd give an Italian, Swiss, or Spanish vendor my money and hope this time the treat would surprise me with some wonderful new flavor. But after a year of throwing away perhaps a dozen purchases, I finally got smart and stopped trying. I just kept wondering, "Don't these people know that a little salt would bring out the flavor and make these foods absolutely delicious?"

Jesus says that we—his followers—are the salt of the earth. We bring the true flavor of life—a life of hope in Christ—to everyone we touch. But if we lose our saltiness, we become like those who do not know Christ. When we begin to process our circumstances and trials through a humanistic worldview, we start to cry out, "This isn't fair! I'm not happy. There must be more. What happened to my life?"

When we focus on our discontentment rather than God's promises, we lose our power . . . our saltiness. Jesus says, in essence, that without our saltiness, we are of no value in the world. In fact, we become a hindrance to those who need Christ. If the love, peace, and joy of following Christ are not oozing from our lives, who will want to know our God?

There is a wonderful cure for a life of discontentment or mediocre complacency. The cure is waking up each morning and reporting for duty to God, who always has a "salty" assignment to flavor your day. Matthew 9:36–38 says:

199

> When he [Jesus] saw the crowds, he had compassion on them, because they were harassed and helpless, like sheep without a shepherd. Then he said to his disciples, "The harvest is plentiful but the workers are few. Ask the Lord of the harvest, therefore, to send out workers into his harvest field."

If your life is lacking passion, go out to the harvest. Share the love of Christ in word and action. There is no greater cure for discontentment than sharing the good news. You have the cure for the cancer of the soul; don't withhold it from anyone.

Prayer

Heavenly Father, please forgive me for the times I have lost my saltiness. Return to me the joy of my salvation so I may share your love with great joy with those who do not know you. I pray for a new passion and purpose to recognize each of your divine assignments and fulfill your purpose in my life. Amen.

Worship

_____

_____

_____

Confession

_____

_____

_____

Thankfulness

_____

_____

_____

Prayer Requests

_____

_____

_____

- From the devotion above I have identified the lie I believe:

  _____

  _____

- The truth I now receive: _____

  _____

  _____

- I practiced healthy biblical self-talk today:
  ☐　　☐　　☐

- My key personal statement is:_____

  _____

  _____

- I have repeated that message at least three times today:
  ☐　　☐　　☐

- I have written my personal statement above or on an index card so I can continue to read it if I need renewal in this area.
☐

- Today I am learning to be more content and joyful by: ____

_____

_____

Day 19 Every Single Word?

But I tell you that men will have to give account on the day of judgment for every careless word they have spoken. For by your words you will be acquitted, and by your words you will be condemned.

Matthew 12:36–37

It amazes me how many people have become "celebrities" by allowing cameras into their lives to record every single thing they say and do. Sadly, the cameras don't seem to temper either. There is an eternal recording in heaven of you. Every careless word you have spoken, muttered, or yelled will be judged by God. That fact is chilling and should remind us daily how important our words are to the Lord.

Our words are powerful whether they are thought, spoken, or written. They can build up, or they can tear down. James 3:9–10 says, "With the tongue we praise our Lord and Father, and with it we curse men, who have been made in God's likeness. Out of the same mouth come praise and cursing. My brothers, this should not be."

Sometimes we live this life as if heaven doesn't exist or what we say or do here on earth will not matter for eternity because we are saved by grace. Our work in this life and the next is to glorify God.

And our words can be a beautiful song of praise or an ugly bellowing of contempt.

My friend Sylvia and I had some unpleasant words with each other a while back. Our rough patch did not last long because we value our friendship. But I can still remember a few of the things she said to me, and I'm sure she remembers those I said to her that did not build her up. We will both be judged for those words.

I once heard it said, "Don't let your manner or your method dilute your message." How we communicate is as important as the words we choose. Since it is our purpose to bring glory to God and to be salt and light to a fallen world, we need to remind ourselves constantly of the importance of our communication. In truth, the words that flow freely are a reflection of our heart. Jesus said it beautifully: "For out of the overflow of the heart the mouth speaks. The good man brings good things out of the good stored up in him, and the evil man brings evil things out of the evil stored up in him" (Matt. 12:34–35).

Prayer

Heavenly Father, please put a guard on my tongue and help me to consider every word before it flows from my mouth. Purify my heart so that good things can flow from me and bring glory to you. Amen.

Worship

_____

_____

_____

Confession

_____

_____

_____

Thankfulness

_____

_____

_____

Prayer Requests

_____

_____

_____

- From the devotion above I have identified the lie I believe:

  _____

  _____

- The truth I now receive: _____

  _____

  _____

- I practiced healthy biblical self-talk today:
  ☐   ☐   ☐

- My key personal statement is:_____

  _____

  _____

- I have repeated that message at least three times today:
  ☐   ☐   ☐

- I have written my personal statement above or on an index card
  so I can continue to read it if I need renewal in this area.
  ☐

- Today I am learning to be more content and joyful by: _____

  _____

  _____

Day 20 Heavenly Inventory

For the Son of Man is going to come in his Father's glory with his angels,
and then he will reward each person according to what he has done.

Matthew 16:27

How long was your to-do list this week? Did you get everything
done? I sure didn't. Perhaps like me, you were busy every day with
little time for relaxation. Think back over the last seven days and
try to account for all you did that could possibly merit a heavenly
reward. What made a difference for eternity? I hope I did at least
one thing each day that mattered to God. But I fear that many days
I failed. Some of us think we need to be an evangelist like Billy
Graham or an angel of mercy like Mother Teresa to earn heavenly
rewards. But God gives us all plenty of divine appointments to touch

another life in meaningful ways. I love what Randy Alcorn writes in his book *Heaven*:

> How many times have we done small acts of kindness on Earth without realizing the effects? How many times have we shared Christ with people we thought didn't take it to heart but who years later came to Jesus partly because of the seeds we planted? How many times have we spoken up for unborn children and seen no result, but as a result someone chose not to have an abortion and saved a child's life? How many dishes have been washed and diapers changed and crying children sung to in the middle of the night, when we couldn't see the impact of the love we showed? And how many times have we seen no response, but God was still pleased with our efforts? God is watching. He is keeping track. In Heaven he'll reward us for our acts of faithfulness to him, right down to every cup of cold water we've given to the needy in his name.[1]

In recent years, God has laid a heavy burden on my heart to reach out to children in third world countries through a partnership with World Vision—a Christian, international, hunger relief organization. After speaking about the child sponsorship as a radio host, I was moved to sponsor several children. When I realized how many children needed help, I began to share their plight every time I spoke at women's retreats and conferences. In the last few years, hundreds of children have been sponsored. You and I can't save all the children, but we can make a difference in the life of one or two. Because many of the World Vision children get to hear and respond to the gospel, I am excited that one day I may meet many of them in heaven.

This past January, God gave me a little glimpse of what I can expect when I met a young man from Zimbabwe. He shared his story of losing his father to terrorist rebels and being saved from a life of violence by becoming a sponsored child. Today, he is a pastor in Virginia who passionately serves the God he learned about as a young boy in Africa.

Our hearts need to break over the things that break the heart of God. When we act on those things, our immediate reward is knowing our actions warm the heart of God. But our actions also have an eternal heavenly reward. How is your heavenly inventory so far?

Prayer

Dear Lord, I don't want to miss your daily opportunities to make an investment for eternity. Please help me to keep my eyes and heart open to ways to give of my time, gifts, and resources that have eternal significance. Amen.

Worship

_____

_____

_____

Confession

_____

_____

_____

Thankfulness

_____

_____

_____

Prayer Requests

_____

_____

_____

- From the devotion above I have identified the lie I believe:

  _____

  _____

- The truth I now receive: _____

  _____

  _____

- I practiced healthy biblical self-talk today:
  ☐　　☐　　☐

- My key personal statement is:_____

  _____

  _____

- I have repeated that message at least three times today:
  ☐　　☐　　☐

- I have written my personal statement above or on an index card
  so I can continue to read it if I need renewal in this area.
  ☐

- Today I am learning to be more content and joyful by: _____

_____

_____

Day 21 What's in It for *Me?*

Peter answered him, "We have left everything to follow you! What then will there be for us?"

Matthew 19:27

You've heard stories about people who invested every cent they had to pursue a dream and in the end lost everything. Many women have tried everything possible to have a baby, only to fail and live out their lives childless. We all have passions, hopes, and dreams we feel compelled to pursue. Sadly, many dreams are never realized, and failure abounds. Even when people dream big dreams and succeed, they must leave it all behind at death. This life is important . . . but the next is paramount. This life will offer some joy and reward. But it will also bring great pain and loss. There is only one guaranteed success in life—to let go of everything and follow Christ.

In today's Scripture passage, Peter's humanity expresses itself when he asks, "What then will there be for us?" The twelve disciples had left everything behind to follow Christ, and Peter wants to know . . . was it worth the cost? If we measure our reward only in terms of this lifetime, perhaps it is not. But as I've said before, *this* life is only a speck of sand in the ocean of eternity. If we don't learn to see life through spiritual eyes, being acutely aware that we are investing for eternity, we will miss many opportunities to receive eternal rewards.

The reality of heavenly rewards seems to contradict the fact that we cannot earn our salvation. If this is true, why would God want us to work for greater rewards in heaven? I certainly cannot speak for God, but I do know he cares deeply about how we live our lives. And while we cannot earn our salvation, James makes it clear that how we live matters: "You foolish man, do you want evidence that faith without deeds is useless?" (2:20). And again in verse 26 he says, "As the body without the spirit is dead, so faith without deeds is dead." He is saying that what we do and how we live this life on earth matter greatly.

In his book *Heaven*, Randy Alcorn sheds greater insight into the importance of our daily works and their potential heavenly rewards. He writes:

> The first judgment is not to be confused with the final judgment, or what is called the judgment of works. The Bible indicates that all believers will stand before the judgment seat of Christ to give an account of their lives. . . . It is critical to understand that this judgment is a judgment of works, not of faith. Our works do not affect our salvation, but they do affect our reward. . . . Christ-centered righteous living today is directly affected by knowing where we're going and what rewards we'll receive there for serving Christ.[1]

Jesus tells his followers that their sacrifice of giving up all their worldly goods and following him will be well rewarded.

> I tell you the truth, at the renewal of all things, when the Son of Man sits on his glorious throne, you who have followed me will also sit on twelve thrones, judging the twelve tribes of Israel. And everyone who has left houses or brothers or sisters or father or mother or children or fields for my sake will receive a hundred times as much and will inherit eternal life. But many who are first will be last, and many who are last will be first.

Matthew 19:28–30

Prayer

Dear God, thank you for showing me that how I live each day matters. Help me to remember that I need to serve you first. And when the draw of this world sucks me in, remind me that my true reward is in heaven with you. Amen.

Worship

_____

_____

_____

Confession

_____

_____

_____

Thankfulness

_____

_____

_____

Prayer Requests

_____

_____

_____

- From the devotion above I have identified the lie I believe:

  _____

  _____

- The truth I now receive: _____

  _____

  _____

- I practiced healthy biblical self-talk today:
  ☐　　　☐　　　☐

- My key personal statement is:_____

  _____

  _____

- I have repeated that message at least three times today:
  ☐　　　☐　　　☐

- I have written my personal statement above or on an index card
  so I can continue to read it if I need renewal in this area.
  ☐

- Today I am learning to be more content and joyful by: _____

_____

_____

Day 22 Forever Satisfied

Then Jesus declared, "I am the bread of life. He who comes to me will never go hungry, and he who believes in me will never be thirsty."

John 6:35

We all get hungry and thirsty every day. The fact that our bodies need continual nourishment and hydration is a powerful reminder of how weak we are and how dependent we are on God's resources to sustain us. Of course, in the passage above, Jesus is speaking of spiritual food and water that will satisfy us fully and sustain us eternally. Just as our bodies hunger and thirst for sustenance, so do our souls. As we live the ups and downs of this life, our spiritual hunger and thirst increase, and we reach out to God to meet our needs.

The psalms are a beautiful place to watch hungry hearts become transformed by God's love and truth. When our souls are starving and thirsty, we must run to the Word and flood our minds with life-giving hope. The words of the psalmists can become our words as we cry out to God from deep within. Psalm 63 is a beautiful expression of one who is seeking God with his whole heart and clinging to him with all his might. A few of my favorite verses feed my soul and I hope do yours as well:

> O God, you are my God,
>   earnestly I seek you;
> my soul thirsts for you. . . .

Because your love is better than life,
    my lips will glorify you. . . .
My soul will be satisfied as with the richest of foods;
    with singing lips my mouth will praise you. . . .
Because you are my help,
    I sing in the shadow of your wings.

vv. 1, 3, 5, 7

When we truly believe that God's love is better than life, our perspective about the life we are encountering today changes. We can fight against our circumstance or we can give in, fall into the shadow of his wings, and stop struggling once and for all.

I love these words the psalmist speaks because it is such a beautiful contrast between our need and God's power. He writes, "My soul clings to You; Your right hand upholds me" (63:8 NASB). We reach out to God in our pain and cling to him, and his right hand of power holds us with a security that will never fail. Cling to God; cling to his truth. Your heart will change, and your soul will consistently sing praises.

You have made known to me the path of life;
    you will fill me with joy in your presence,
    with eternal pleasures at your right hand.
Psalm 16:11

Prayer

God of power and refuge, I cling to you in my weakness and despair. I need you in the good times and the bad. I pray you will make your presence known to me even when I am weak with doubt. Transform my heart so that the outflow of my mouth will be the praises you deserve. Amen.

Worship

_____

_____

_____

Confession

_____

_____

_____

Thankfulness

_____

_____

_____

Prayer Requests

_____

_____

_____

- From the devotion above I have identified the lie I believe:

_____

_____

- The truth I now receive: _____

  _____

  _____

- I practiced healthy biblical self-talk today:

  ☐   ☐   ☐

- My key personal statement is:_____

  _____

  _____

- I have repeated that message at least three times today:

  ☐   ☐   ☐

- I have written my personal statement above or on an index card so I can continue to read it if I need renewal in this area.

  ☐

- Today I am learning to be more content and joyful by: ____

  _____

  _____

Day 23 Letting Go

Jesus answered, "If you want to be perfect, go, sell your possessions and give to the poor, and you will have treasure in heaven. Then come, follow me." When the young man heard this, he went away sad, because he had great wealth.

Matthew 19:21–22

Waterskiing requires great timing, balance, and knowing when to let go. When I was younger, I was pretty good at skiing on one ski. It was so much fun to cut across the wake from the boat and lean as far to one side as I could as I skimmed across the surface of the lake. That's the picture I had in mind when I decided to give it a try again a few years ago.

I'm relatively athletic, and I figured I'd just pop out of the water like I did in my younger years. So I yelled, "Hit it!" but things didn't go as planned. I tried again and again . . . and still I did not pop out of the water. With fierce determination, I decided to give it one more try. I was not letting go of the rope handle this time. I was going to get up on one ski if it killed me. It nearly did. The next thing I heard (and felt) was a loud pop, and I was down. When we don't follow simple principles of nature, something has got to give. This time, it was my hamstring. I not only failed to ski that day, but I also lost my ability to walk for a while. My muscle was torn so badly that I had black and purple bruising from the top of my thigh to my ankle. My leg was swollen, and my ego was deflated.

Sometimes, we need to let go. Let go of our fears. Let go of our false security blankets. Let go of our pride. Let go of absolutely everything that gets in the way of fully surrendering our life to Christ. There is a price to pay when we don't. In the verse above, a rich young man who knows the Lord's commandments and follows most of them wants to know what he must *do* to earn eternal life. Of course, we know that working our way to heaven requires absolute perfection, which is utterly impossible. In this man's case, the thing he lacked was his willingness to let go of his riches. When Jesus told him to sell his possessions, give to the poor, and follow him, the man went away sad because he loved his wealth more than he loved Christ. He couldn't let go, and the eternal consequence was certainly not worth the riches he held so tightly in his fists.

God loves us beyond measure—so much that he gave his only Son to die for us. He held back nothing to deliver us from our sin and selfishness, and he wants nothing less than all of us. Letting go is incredibly hard when we think we know what will fulfill us. At first, complete surrender may feel as if you are free-falling without a parachute. But it's actually the safest jump you will ever take—directly into the loving arms of God, who rewards you with deep joy and contentment.

Prayer

Father God, I want to trust you with my entire life, yet my actions often show that I do not. I sometimes live as if I want to keep my feet in two worlds and reap the benefit of both. Please help me let go of the things of this world and follow you with all my heart. Amen.

Worship

_____

_____

_____

Confession

_____

_____

_____

Thankfulness

_____

_____

_____

Prayer Requests

_____

_____

_____

- From the devotion above I have identified the lie I believe:

  _____

  _____

- The truth I now receive: _____

  _____

  _____

- I practiced healthy biblical self-talk today:
  ☐   ☐   ☐

- My key personal statement is:_____

  _____

  _____

- I have repeated that message at least three times today:
  ☐   ☐   ☐

- I have written my personal statement above or on an index card so I can continue to read it if I need renewal in this area.
  ☐

- Today I am learning to be more content and joyful by: ____

  _____

  _____

Day 24 Divine Possibilities

Jesus looked at them and said, "With man this is impossible, but with God all things are possible."

Matthew 19:26

With God all things are possible. Don't you just love the sound of that? And it is so true. Yet, we better be careful how we apply that truth to our lives because it is not a promise that God will always do the impossible when we ask. Just because we think something is good does not mean he will move in his mighty power to accomplish what we desire. It is our job to seek his will, to let our requests be made known, and to accept his answer, for in addition to being all-powerful, he is all-knowing. Because his knowledge is complete, all his actions are based on full wisdom. We can be sure everything he does is the right thing.

My son, Jesse, spent his fourth- and fifth-grade years in Lugano, Switzerland, at the American School with students from all over the world. The experience was both good and bad. The good was obvious; he was introduced to many new places and cultures. The bad was all about perspective and value. Most of the people in Lugano worshiped money. Jesse's friends were driven to school in limos, they took outrageously expensive vacations, and at ten years of age, many wore Rolex watches and sported iTouch phones. Jesse thought it was so unfair that he could not have these things. He asked me if we were rich, would I buy them for him. I told him, "Absolutely not!" Even if it were possible, it was not going to happen. My job is to give my son what he needs, not what he wants! Thankfully, we moved back to San Diego before Jesse started his sixth-grade year. He's back in a Christian school with his feet on the ground and his eyes on the Lord.

When Jesus spoke the words, "With God all things are possible," the rich man we spoke about yesterday had just walked away in sadness. The Lord told his disciples that it was hard for a rich man to enter the kingdom of heaven. He shocked them when he emphasized his point by saying that it was easier for a camel to go through the eye of a needle—an impossible feat. The men were dismayed and wondered, if this were true, who could make it to heaven. Jesus needed to make it abundantly clear that except for the grace of God, it was impossible for anyone to be saved. He was pointing forward to his impending death and resurrection, which would make the impossible possible!

We cannot save ourselves. We can try to follow all the rules, striving for ultimate perfection, but we will never make it. It is only by the blood of Christ that we can be saved. As a believer, you are a living, breathing miracle! God has already done the impossible in your life. And the same grace that saves us from our sins also does the impossible by slowly but surely transforming us into the image of Christ.

Prayer

Father God, thank you for doing the impossible in my life. I already have all that I need knowing that all your riches are stored up for me in heaven, where I will spend eternity with you. Please help me to know your will for my life and to pray in accordance with that will. Give me eyes to see those who desperately need you, and help me to be a light in the darkness for them, pointing them to the blood of Christ. Amen.

Worship

_____

_____

_____

Confession

_____

_____

_____

Thankfulness

_____

_____

_____

Prayer Requests

_____

_____

_____

- From the devotion above I have identified the lie I believe:

  _____

  _____

- The truth I now receive: _____

  _____

  _____

- I practiced healthy biblical self-talk today:

  ☐   ☐   ☐

- My key personal statement is:_____

  _____

  _____

- I have repeated that message at least three times today:

  ☐   ☐   ☐

- I have written my personal statement above or on an index card
  so I can continue to read it if I need renewal in this area.

  ☐

- Today I am learning to be more content and joyful by: _____

  _____

  _____

Day 25 Rest for the Weary

Come to me, all you who are weary and burdened, and I will give you rest. Take my yoke upon you and learn from me, for I am gentle and humble in heart, and you will find rest for your souls. For my yoke is easy and my burden is light.

Matthew 11:28–30

Popcorn and a really good movie can get my mind off all the stresses and strains of life . . . until the movie is over. Then it's back to reality, and the benefit of the momentary distraction vanishes like a morning mist.

It is amazing how our human default mechanism often exacerbates our problems. Our misery factor flies off the charts when we don't see each day's challenges in the proper perspective. When I am wearied and burdened by the usual day-to-day pressures, I often realize that I am placing too much importance on everyone's expectations of me—at least what I *think* those expectations are. What does it matter if I buy cupcakes at the bakery instead of baking them myself? Am I an inadequate wife if I serve my family leftovers three days in a row?

All of our negative emotions and words flow out of our thoughts. For most of us, the largest portion of our burden is our worrisome perspective. We need to take a deep breath and realize that we wear ourselves out by stressing over things we cannot change or that won't really make a difference a week from now.

At times I must stop in the middle of my day and simply drop my issues at the feet of Jesus. He alone can give me the right perspective. When I read verse 28 above, I imagine a heavy wooden yoke across my shoulders—the tension in my shoulders verifies that I've been carrying it way too long. I can see Jesus lifting it off me and setting it down. As he does, I feel the muscles in my body relax. He invites me to sit next to him on a grassy knoll and tells me how much he loves me. He speaks of heaven and how the pain and burdens of this world will pass away. He reminds me that even the greatest tragedies I may face here will one day seem small in the light of his grace. In that moment of surrender and rest for my soul, I am recentered and energized to face the rest of the day with Jesus by my side—carrying my burden and tilting my chin heavenward.

Prayer

Lord, I need you to take my heavy yoke and lighten the load in my soul. I know that can happen only when I shift my focus from this world to the next and see things in the right perspective. Even when I am carrying more than a person should carry, I know you can bring rest to my soul. Show me how to sit with you for a few precious moments throughout each day to get the strength I need to carry on. Amen.

Worship

_____

_____

_____

Confession

_____

_____

_____

Thankfulness

_____

_____

_____

Prayer Requests

_____

_____

_____

- From the devotion above I have identified the lie I believe:

  _____

  _____

- The truth I now receive: _____

  _____

  _____

- I practiced healthy biblical self-talk today:
  ☐   ☐   ☐

- My key personal statement is:_____

  _____

  _____

- I have repeated that message at least three times today:
  ☐   ☐   ☐

- I have written my personal statement above or on an index card so I can continue to read it if I need renewal in this area.
  ☐

- Today I am learning to be more content and joyful by: ____

  _____

  _____

Day 26 Set Free

If you hold to my teaching, you are really my disciples. Then you will know the truth, and the truth will set you free.

John 8:31–32

A young woman asked my advice about trading in a car that was clearly on its last legs or, more accurately, last wheels. She was cash poor and knew that many car dealers were making great offers because of the current economic climate. Her car would be difficult to sell in its current condition, and she had no cash to fix it, but she knew she could trade it in and get an affordable and reliable used car for about five thousand dollars. Taking on any debt requires careful consideration, and debt must be kept to a minimum even for something as important as a car. I encouraged her to set the maximum price and monthly payment in her mind and refuse to move beyond it. It is amazing how motivated a car salesmen can be if you are ready to walk out the door.

Sadly, the salesman got the better of her and offered her the same modest payments per month for a car that would put her ten thousand dollars in debt rather than five thousand dollars. Of course, she'd be making those payments much longer. The lure of the nicer car right now was greater than the reality of keeping her debt low. In that moment, she cared more about her current comfort than the lingering stress of paying off double the debt. Instead of taking my advice, she followed her emotions and rationalized the debt by saying, "I can totally afford the payments!" She became a servant to her emotions and her lender.

Jesus tells us in the passage above that we prove ourselves to be his followers when we actually follow his advice. We can say we believe the Bible holds all of life's answers. We can say we love the Lord and want to give him every aspect of our life. We can say a lot of things, but if our actions do not follow, we are simply spouting hot air.

If we believe God has a perfect plan for our life, as he teaches in his Word, then why don't we follow it? Like the young woman in the illustration above, we let emotions or immediate gratification lead us rather than truth. I once heard a wise man say, "I'd rather be a hypocrite to my emotions than to the Word of God." If we want true freedom, we find it by living the principles of Christ in the details of our daily life.

Prayer

Heavenly Father, your wisdom is the only truth I need to guide me through life. Please forgive me when I care more about my gratification than your glorification. Please speak to my heart when I am tempted to choose my way over yours. I pray you give me a burning desire not only to know your Word but to follow it. Then I will know your truth in an active way, and you will set me free. Amen.

Worship

Confession

_____

_____

_____

Thankfulness

_____

_____

_____

Prayer Requests

_____

_____

_____

- From the devotion above I have identified the lie I believe:

  _____

  _____

- The truth I now receive: _____

  _____

  _____

- I practiced healthy biblical self-talk today:
  ☐   ☐   ☐

- My key personal statement is:_____

  _____

  _____

- I have repeated that message at least three times today:
  ☐   ☐   ☐

- I have written my personal statement above or on an index card
  so I can continue to read it if I need renewal in this area.
  ☐

- Today I am learning to be more content and joyful by: _____

  _____

  _____

Day 27 God's Perfect Will

Father, if you are willing, take this cup from me; yet not my will, but
yours be done.

Luke 22:42

When difficult times come—and they always do—most of us immediately run to God in prayer. That's a good thing. Before a word
leaves our mouth, he knows our heart's desire. Most of us ask God
to take the trial or painful circumstance away. It is comforting to
know that even Jesus wanted his most difficult trial removed. He
was all God and all man. In his humanness, he felt what we feel—
pain, sorrow, fear. This is evidenced by the fact that his sweat was
"as drops of blood" in those solitary hours of prayer in Gethsemane

when he said to the disciples, "My soul is overwhelmed with sorrow to the point of death" (Mark 14:34). He returned to pray three times before facing his destiny.

Of course, Jesus knew the entire story of his life and purpose from beginning to end—from the unfair trial to his death on a cross to his glorious resurrection. Yet, in the hours before his death, he poured out his heart to God, asking if there was another way to save humankind from their sins. In the same breath that uttered his petition for relief, he also surrendered his entire being to God's perfect will. For that we will be eternally grateful. All of history hinges on Christ's perfect obedience and sacrifice.

God knows we cannot fully understand the scope of his purpose in the trials of life. Our flesh cries out for comfort and relief. We want immediate deliverance from our despair. God loves us beyond human comprehension. He loves us just as we are with all our warts and flaws. But as it's been said many times, he also loves us too much to leave us where we are. Just as diamonds are perfected in the intense pressure and heat beneath the earth, we are perfected in the difficulties of life. Like Jesus, we can ask for our bitter cup of pain to be removed. Perhaps at times he will do just that. But also like Jesus, we must readily surrender to God's perfect will, knowing that in his will we are shaped into the likeness of his son.

Prayer

Heavenly Father, life is so difficult sometimes. It is easy to forget that life is so much more than the ups and downs we experience for these few short years on earth. Please help me to sense the greater scope of your will working in the trials and tribulations of life. Help me to be more like Jesus and to know when I must endure a trial for a great purpose. Help me to be more like Christ each day. Amen.

Worship

_____

_____

_____

Confession

_____

_____

_____

Thankfulness

_____

_____

_____

Prayer Requests

_____

_____

_____

- From the devotion above I have identified the lie I believe:

  _____

  _____

- The truth I now receive: _____

  _____

  _____

- I practiced healthy biblical self-talk today:

  ☐   ☐   ☐

- My key personal statement is:_____

  _____

  _____

- I have repeated that message at least three times today:

  ☐   ☐   ☐

- I have written my personal statement above or on an index card so I can continue to read it if I need renewal in this area.

  ☐

- Today I am learning to be more content and joyful by: _____

  _____

  _____

Day 28 The Hands and Feet of Christ

"Lord, when did we see you hungry and feed you, or thirsty and give you something to drink? When did we see you a stranger and invite you in, or needing clothes and clothe you? When did we see you sick or in prison and go to visit you?" The King will reply, "I tell you the truth, whatever you did for one of the least of these brothers of mine, you did for me."

Matthew 25:37–40

The Lord cares deeply about the poor, weak, downtrodden, and oppressed. When we reach out and meet others' needs, he says it is as if we were doing it unto him. Not only do we bless another person who is perhaps less fortunate than ourselves, but we also change our focus. One surefire way to get your mind off your own troubles is to redirect it to someone else's.

We all remember where we were the morning of September 11, 2001. Fear gripped our nation as we watched the devastation two jets caused by flying into the twin towers in New York City. As another plane crashed into the Pentagon and yet another into a field in Pennsylvania, we were dumbstruck. In the hours and days following the shock and horror of being terrorized on our own soil, few Americans complained about their minor aches and pains, lack of sleep, problems with family members, or other assorted life difficulties. All over the country, people reached out to one another in compassion and sympathy. Letters and prayers poured out to the grieving people left behind. We imagined what it would be like if we had been there. We all experienced a reality check, and most of us thanked God for our families and friends. Everyone became keenly aware that life in a fallen world is fragile.

Yet, as disturbing as 9/11 was, we must realize that each day holds tragedy for many around the globe. Every three seconds a child dies from hunger or a hunger-related disease somewhere in the world. Men and women are diagnosed with cancer every day. Sons and daughters sacrifice their lives for our country.

Loss and pain are everywhere . . . and God cares deeply. For a short time, he is allowing the sin of humankind to manifest itself in dire consequences. In the midst of all this pain, Jesus calls us to feed the hungry, give water to the thirsty, clothe the poor, and comfort the downhearted. If you are looking for deep satisfaction in your life—even in the midst of your own pain or tragedy—look up and out. Extend your hand and heart to one who is hurting even more than you. Fulfilling needs fills your heart and touches the heart of God. Don't wait until your life is just so before you reach out. Reach out today . . . reach out every day . . . in big and small ways. It will change your life.

Prayer

Father God, you are the one who brings us hope and comfort. I pray you will use me to be the hands and heart of Jesus to those who are hurting in this world. The needs are so great, and it seems I have so little to give. Please show me what I can do to help another in distress. Amen.

Worship

_____

_____

_____

Confession

_____

_____

_____

Thankfulness

_____

_____

_____

Prayer Requests

_____

_____

_____

- From the devotion above I have identified the lie I believe:

  _____

  _____

- The truth I now receive: _____

  _____

  _____

- I practiced healthy biblical self-talk today:
  ☐   ☐   ☐

- My key personal statement is:_____

  _____

  _____

- I have repeated that message at least three times today:
  ☐   ☐   ☐

- I have written my personal statement above or on an index card so I can continue to read it if I need renewal in this area.

  ☐

- Today I am learning to be more content and joyful by: ____

  _____

  _____

Day 29 Forever Forgiving

Then Peter came to Jesus and asked, "Lord, how many times shall I forgive my brother when he sins against me? Up to seven times?" Jesus answered, "I tell you, not seven times, but seventy-seven times."

Matthew 18:21–22

Some things are easier to forgive than others. An unkind word, a careless action, or an occasional act of disrespect can be forgiven much more readily than a heartbreaking betrayal. When my husband betrayed me with another woman, it would have been easy to make him beg for months for forgiveness. Yet, God showed me an image of Christ on the cross, hanging there for my sins. Jesus never said, "Danna, I won't die for that sin. That one is unforgiveable." He didn't withhold his mercy and grace from one sin, big or small. He paid the price for them all—past, present, *and* future. How could I withhold forgiveness from my husband for even one day?

Are you willing to pursue others in the same way God pursues you? Are you willing to forgive, restore, and reconcile as he has? Everyone is emotionally vulnerable. We are not as strong as we think. We are all capable of dark and damaging behaviors given the right circumstances. First Corinthians 10:12 says, "So, if you think you are standing firm, be careful that you don't fall!"

God forgives even though we grieve his Holy Spirit with our defiant and rebellious behavior. His love prevails even though we experience a time of interrupted fellowship as his loving discipline guides us back home. Let us learn from him as we set healthy yet loving boundaries for the prodigals in our lives, always ready to embrace them even in the midst of their darkest hour.

Hopefully when you fail and then reach out for reconciliation, a loving person will grab on tightly and pull you toward truth. If you want to be a reconciler, you need to believe that no one can go too far. If you extend the same grace to others in your life, it will never be too late for them to reconcile with you. Consider the words of the apostle Paul to the Colossians: "Clothe yourselves with compassion, kindness, humility, gentleness and patience. Bear with each other and forgive whatever grievances you may have against one another. Forgive as the Lord forgave you" (3:12–13).

If our heavenly Father, the creator of heaven and earth, of all that lives and breathes, can extend such mercy to me, how can I withhold mercy from another? So whether that prodigal is my daughter or son, my spouse, my co-worker, or my friend, I forgive and say "come home" again and again. It's never about anyone being worthy. No one is worthy. It's about the fact we are God's children. We need the people in our lives to know that if they are out on a limb and feel there is no place to go, they have not gone too far . . . they can always come home.

Prayer

Father in heaven, thank you for your gift of forgiveness through the blood of your precious Son, Jesus Christ. I will be forever grateful for the mercy and grace you have given me. Please forgive me for the times I have withheld my forgiveness. Help me to act quickly and forgive those who sin against me so they may know it is by your grace alone that I can forgive at all. Praise your holy name. Amen.

Worship

_____

_____

_____

Confession

_____

_____

_____

Thankfulness

_____

_____

_____

Prayer Requests

_____

_____

_____

- From the devotion above I have identified the lie I believe:

  _____

  _____

- The truth I now receive: _____

  _____

  _____

- I practiced healthy biblical self-talk today:
  ☐   ☐   ☐

- My key personal statement is:_____

  _____

  _____

- I have repeated that message at least three times today:
  ☐   ☐   ☐

- I have written my personal statement above or on an index card
  so I can continue to read it if I need renewal in this area.
  ☐

- Today I am learning to be more content and joyful by: _____

  _____

  _____

Day 30 A Heavenly Reservation

In my Father's house are many rooms; if it were not so, I would have told you. I am going there to prepare a place for you. And if I go and prepare a place for you, I will come back and take you to be with me that you also may be where I am.

John 14:2–3

At a recent retreat, I was privileged to share the stage with Don Piper, author of *90 Minutes in Heaven*. In his book, he shares his experience of being pronounced dead at the scene by several emergency medical personnel after being crushed by a semitruck in a horrific head-on collision. Ninety minutes later, he came back to life as a Christian man prayed over his mangled, lifeless body. In those ninety minutes, he had a memorable experience. Don believes he went to heaven, and what he experienced forever changed him. In fact, he was angry and depressed that he had to return to his old life with all its pain and imperfection. In the first year following his accident, Don underwent more than thirty surgeries and lived with excruciating pain. He kept his heavenly visit a secret for almost fifteen years, fearing no one would believe him and considering it his "sacred secret." However, some Christian friends prodded him to tell his story, believing God had given him this experience to encourage others.

When Don speaks, he has a pastoral, comforting presence. I was moved by how he exuded hope to those who had suffered the loss of a loved one. If he was certain the deceased was a believer, he would say, "I am sorry for your temporary separation, but rest assured that your loved one is in an absolutely wonderful place. There is no sense of loss for them because time exists on a different plane. So in their heavenly experience, you will be reunited in a very short while!" Don said that everything he saw and heard during his experience, he found validated in the Bible: the sound of multitudes singing "Holy, holy, holy," gates made of gigantic pearls, and even the streets paved with gold.

Jesus spoke of heaven numerous times in his teaching. In the verses above, he gives us great assurance that he is personally preparing a place for us to dwell with him for eternity. We also know from Paul's teaching in 1 Corinthians 15:35–49 that we will have new, perfect bodies one day. As my mother ages (now eighty) and her pain increases and her mobility decreases, she looks forward to heaven more each day. Whether we are taken at a relatively young age or die in old, decrepit bodies, heaven is not just a pleasant alternative to life . . . it is the ultimate life!

If only we were able to continually process life with "eternal glasses" on, causing us to see our current trials and tribulations accurately. In reality, this life on earth is merely a speck of sand in the ocean of time. Like labor pains, this imperfect life will pass, and we will be delivered to a perfect, eternal life and reunited with those who call Jesus their Savior and with God himself. Have you made your reservation?

Prayer

Oh, Father, what incredible hope and joy you give us by telling us what we can look forward to in heaven. Please forgive me for holding on so tightly to the things of this world. Please help me to see my daily life through eternal lenses that keep me looking toward the real life you have planned for me. Amen.

Worship

_____

_____

_____

Confession

_____
_____
_____

Thankfulness

_____
_____
_____

Prayer Requests

_____
_____
_____

- From the devotion above I have identified the lie I believe:

_____
_____

- The truth I now receive: _____

_____
_____

- I practiced healthy biblical self-talk today:
  ☐   ☐   ☐

- My key personal statement is:_____

  _____

  _____

- I have repeated that message at least three times today:

  ☐   ☐   ☐

- I have written my personal statement above or on an index card
  so I can continue to read it if I need renewal in this area.

  ☐

- Today I am learning to be more content and joyful by: _____

  _____

  _____

Day 31 Fully Loved and Counted

> Are not two sparrows sold for a penny? Yet not one of them will fall
> to the ground apart from the will of your Father. And even the very
> hairs of your head are all numbered. So don't be afraid; you are worth
> more than many sparrows.
>
> Matthew 10:29–31

When I became pregnant for the first time, I spent hours just
imagining how my baby was changing every day. I could barely wait
to meet my unborn child. I was obsessed with learning everything
I could to become a good mother. As a new believer at the time, I
was awestruck reading Psalm 139, especially verses 13 and 16: "For
you created my inmost being; you knit me together in my mother's

womb. . . . Your eyes saw my unformed body. All the days ordained for me were written in your book before one of them came to be." I was mesmerized by the reality that God could see my baby daughter growing inside me—that he already knew everything about her before she was even a reality in my life.

When Jamie was born, I became familiar with every inch of her body. I knew that her right ear was just a tad smaller than her left. A tiny splotch of redness on her back did not go unnoticed. I never knew that I could love so fully and give myself so sacrificially to another human being.

As much as a parent can love a child, our love can never come close to the love God has for each one of us. God not only values us above sparrows and knows the number of hairs on our head, but he also knows every detail about us and is always with us.

We are loved beyond measure, with his perfect, everlasting love. When you feel alone, unworthy, or dissatisfied with life, redirect your focus to how intimately God knows you. Realize that he is constantly with you. Meditate on the powerful opening words of Psalm 139, and then read the entire psalm every day until you know just how much God cares for you.

> O Lord, you have searched me
> and you know me.
> You know when I sit and when I rise;
> you perceive my thoughts from afar.
> You discern my going out and my lying down;
> you are familiar with all my ways.
>
> Psalm 139:1–3

Prayer

Father God, thank you for showing me that your love is intimate and all-encompassing. Knowing that you love me enough to count the hairs on my head gives me great joy. Please help me to realize the fullness of your love in a real way each day so I can embrace this life you have given me with passion and purpose. Amen.

Worship

_____

_____

_____

Confession

_____

_____

_____

Thankfulness

_____

_____

_____

Prayer Requests

_____

_____

_____

- From the devotion above I have identified the lie I believe:

  _____

  _____

- The truth I now receive: _____

  _____

  _____

- I practiced healthy biblical self-talk today:
  ☐   ☐   ☐

- My key personal statement is:_____

  _____

  _____

- I have repeated that message at least three times today:
  ☐   ☐   ☐

- I have written my personal statement above or on an index card
  so I can continue to read it if I need renewal in this area.
  ☐

- Today I am learning to be more content and joyful by: ____

  _____

  _____

Day 32 The Simple Life

> So do not worry, saying, "What shall we eat?" or "What shall we drink?" or "What shall we wear?" For the pagans run after all these things, and your heavenly Father knows that you need them.
>
> Matthew 6:31–32

I read the fictitious story below about an American businessman who spent most of his time and energy striving to amass a great amount of wealth. In his mind, a person could never have too much.

> One day while on vacation, the businessman docked his tourist boat in a tiny Mexican fishing village and proceeded to compliment a Mexican fisherman on the quality of his fish. He asked how long it took to catch them.
>
> "Not very long," answered the Mexican.
>
> "But then, why didn't you stay out longer and catch more?" asked the American. The Mexican explained that his small catch was sufficient to meet his needs and those of his family. The American asked, "But what do you do with the rest of your time?"
>
> "I sleep late, fish a little, play with my children, and take a siesta with my wife. In the evenings, I go into the village to see my friends, play the guitar, and sing a few songs. I have a very full life."
>
> The American interrupted, "I have an MBA from Harvard, and I can help you! You should start by fishing longer every day. You can then sell the extra fish you catch. With the extra revenue, you can buy a bigger boat."
>
> "And after that?" asked the Mexican.
>
> "With the extra money the larger boat will bring, you can buy more boats until you have an entire fleet of trawlers. Instead

248

of selling your fish to a middle man, you can then negotiate directly with the processing plants and maybe even open your own plant. You can then leave this little village and move to Mexico City, Los Angeles, or even New York City! From there you can direct your huge new enterprise."

"How long would that take?" asked the Mexican.

"Twenty, perhaps twenty-five years," replied the American.

"And after that?" asked the fisherman.

"Well, my friend, that's when it gets really interesting," answered the American. "When your business gets really big, you can start selling stocks and make millions!"

"Millions? Really? And after that?" replied the Mexican.

"After that you'll be able to retire, live in a tiny village near the coast, sleep late, play with your children, catch a few fish, take a siesta with your wife, and spend your evenings doing what you like and enjoying your friends!"

Most of us have all we really need for today—we just want more. Like the pagans Jesus spoke about in the Scripture passage for today, we strive for more, not realizing that the lifestyle we gain cannot be fully enjoyed because we are so wrapped up in accumulating and taking care of all our stuff!

Prayer

Father God, please forgive me for sometimes wanting so much more than what I need. Give me a heart of thankfulness and contentment. Help me to celebrate a life of simplicity with great joy. I am thankful that you supply all my needs, Lord. Amen.

Worship

_____

_____

_____

Confession

_____

_____

_____

Thankfulness

_____

_____

_____

Prayer Requests

_____

_____

_____

- From the devotion above I have identified the lie I believe:

_____

_____

- The truth I now receive: _____

  _____

  _____

- I practiced healthy biblical self-talk today:
  ☐   ☐   ☐

- My key personal statement is:_____

  _____

  _____

- I have repeated that message at least three times today:
  ☐   ☐   ☐

- I have written my personal statement above or on an index card
  so I can continue to read it if I need renewal in this area.
  ☐

- Today I am learning to be more content and joyful by: _____

  _____

  _____

Day 33 Leap of Faith

He replied, "You of little faith, why are you so afraid?" Then he got up
and rebuked the winds and the waves, and it was completely calm.

Matthew 8:26

Do you have a personal relationship with Christ and yet still live in fear? Have you had a crisis of faith and wondered, "How can I trust God with every detail of my life?" Most people experience fear from time to time. In those moments, we need to redirect ourselves to the substance of our faith and remind ourselves why we believe what we believe.

When our pastor, Tim, was much younger and concerned about making good impressions, he was baited into skydiving with a group of people. He didn't want to seem like a chicken, so he joined them for jump school, hoping he could figure out a way to avoid the actual jump later. After an hour of training, the petite, female instructor announced that it was time to jump. Tim was too embarrassed to shrink away, so he put on the orange jumpsuit and helmet and boarded the plane. When his time came to jump, the instructor yelled, "Go!" and he yelled back, "Wait! How do I know *for sure* that there's a parachute back there and not a sleeping bag or something?"

She replied, barely suppressing her irritation, "There *is* a parachute back there. Is *that* what you are worried about?"

"Well, yeah . . . that and . . . dying!" he replied.

Sensing Tim's serious lack of faith, she got serious as well. "Listen," she answered in a calm and compassionate voice, "I've been a jumpmaster for over twenty years. I'm certified to pack parachutes. I've packed thousands. There's a seal on that chute. That's *my* seal. My seal, my twenty years, my experience . . . *that's* how you know there's a chute that's going to open on your back!"

Suddenly Tim's entire perspective changed. He had confidence there was a parachute and it would open. He jumped, it opened, and he landed safely. That's faith. A credible source speaks, and we accept it. If there is no communication, there is no substance to our faith. God is our jumpmaster. He's not asking us to take a leap without a parachute. We may not see the parachute or understand how it was designed and packed. But we trust the one who tells us it is safe to act.

Prayer

Lord, please help me to have unfaltering faith when life gets difficult. I know in my mind that you are sovereign and in control, yet I still have fear and worry. Please forgive me for this and replace my fear with faith so I can trust you completely even in the most severe storms of life. Amen.

Worship

_____

_____

_____

Confession

_____

_____

_____

Thankfulness

_____

_____

_____

Prayer Requests

_____

_____

_____

- From the devotion above I have identified the lie I believe:

  _____

  _____

- The truth I now receive: _____

  _____

  _____

- I practiced healthy biblical self-talk today:
  ☐   ☐   ☐

- My key personal statement is:_____

  _____

  _____

- I have repeated that message at least three times today:
  ☐   ☐   ☐

- I have written my personal statement above or on an index card
  so I can continue to read it if I need renewal in this area.
  ☐

- Today I am learning to be more content and joyful by:

_____

_____

Day 34 Everything

But a poor widow came and put in two very small copper coins, worth only a fraction of a penny. Calling his disciples to him, Jesus said, "I tell you the truth, this poor widow has put more into the treasury than all the others. They all gave out of their wealth; but she, out of her poverty, put in everything—all she had to live on."

Mark 12:42–44

"Ten percent . . . is that of net or gross?" the businessman asked the pastor regarding his message on the biblical concept of tithing. Perhaps we are missing the entire point of giving back to God if we must ask questions like that. The truth is, God does not *need* our money. But he does tell us to give to the poor and to support the ministry of the gospel. How we respond to those commands reveals a lot about our relationship with him.

In his book *Money, Possessions, and Eternity*, Randy Alcorn makes some powerful and convicting statements about this very subject. He writes:

There's a battle over ownership and lordship of our lives that's just as intense as the battle for salvation. The grace that saves us is also the grace that sanctifies us and empowers us. God's power isn't just needed by unbelievers to be converted. It's needed by believers to be obedient and joyful.[1]

As believers, our level of joy and contentment is directly related to our obedience to the Lord in all areas of life. One of the best ways to test your love for God is to evaluate your attitude about giving. If you truly recognize that everything you have is his and give back to him joyfully, you can be sure that you are choosing to put him first in your life. Sacrificial giving reflects a heart of faith and trust that the Lord is indeed the giver of all good things and will meet us in our need.

Prayer

Heavenly Father, forgive me for the times I have not been obedient to you in giving from that which you have given me. I want to be a joyful giver who trusts you to provide. Please increase my faith and obedience. Amen.

Worship

_____

_____

_____

Confession

_____

_____

_____

Thankfulness

_____

_____

_____

Prayer Requests

_____

_____

_____

- From the devotion above I have identified the lie I believe:

_____

_____

- The truth I now receive: _____

_____

_____

- I practiced healthy biblical self-talk today:
  ☐   ☐   ☐

- My key personal statement is:_____

_____

_____

- I have repeated that message at least three times today:
  ☐   ☐   ☐

- I have written my personal statement above or on an index card so I can continue to read it if I need renewal in this area.

  ☐

- Today I am learning to be more content and joyful by:

  _____

  _____

Day 35 Where Is Your Treasure?

For where your treasure is, there your heart will be also.

Matthew 6:21

With the exception of two wonderful years in Europe, we have lived in our home in San Diego for eighteen years. Our next-door neighbors are dear friends whom we consider family. My parents (now in their eighties) live one block away. We would love to live here the rest of our lives (Lord willing).

Over the years, we have invested a lot of money in not only maintaining our home but also improving it. It is not the same dwelling we bought all those years ago. The more we invest financially, the more we become invested emotionally as well. Our home reflects our personality and style. It is the place where we build family memories. We are thankful to God that he has entrusted us with it and that my husband has maintained a job in this crazy economy. Each month we thank the Lord for the income to pay our mortgage and bills and for the privilege of living in our lovely home for another thirty days!

As much as we love our house, we know it is a temporary home. Our real home will be in heaven. If we invest what God has given us only on the things of this earth, we will have nothing of eternal value stored up. Jesus teaches us that our heart follows our treasure. When we give to our local church, our connection increases, and we gain a greater sense of responsibility and care for the ministry there. When we give to the poor, our heart becomes attached to them, and our compassion grows for those who have so much less than we have. When we are deeply grateful for all God has provided and realize it is not ours, we hold everything with an open hand and can give from a heart filled with thanks. I love what Brennan Manning writes in *Ruthless Trust*:

> The foremost quality of a trusting disciple is gratefulness. Gratitude arises from the lived perception, evaluation, and acceptance of all of life as grace—as an undeserved and unearned gift from the Father's hand.[1]

If you want to love God and his people more, put your treasure where it can make an impact. Where is your heart invested?

Prayer

Lord, I want my heart to be fully connected to you and the things that matter to you. Increase my faith and trust that I may invest my treasure—that which you have provided—somewhere that makes an eternal impact. Amen.

Worship

_____

_____

_____

Confession

_____

_____

_____

Thankfulness

_____

_____

_____

Prayer Requests

_____

_____

_____

- From the devotion above I have identified the lie I believe:

  _____

  _____

- The truth I now receive: _____

  _____

  _____

- I practiced healthy biblical self-talk today:
  ☐   ☐   ☐

- My key personal statement is:_____

  _____

  _____

- I have repeated that message at least three times today:

  ☐   ☐   ☐

- I have written my personal statement above or on an index card

  so I can continue to read it if I need renewal in this area.

  ☐

- Today I am learning to be more content and joyful by: ____

  _____

  _____

Day 36 Do unto Others

Do not judge, and you will not be judged. Do not condemn, and you
will not be condemned. Forgive, and you will be forgiven. Give, and
it will be given to you.

Luke 6:37–38

"Who are you to give us advice about our lives and how to raise
our children?" the man angrily shouted at his brother-in-law before
continuing with his harsh and condemning tirade. "Your children are
inconsiderate and rebellious. You're a failure as a father and have no
right to share your opinions with me." Harsh words and harsh judgment spewed from a man who clearly believed he was more "righteous"
than the other. Perhaps he had done some things better, but Jesus is

clear that it is not our job to judge one another. On occasion, illegal or immoral behavior must be judged in a court of law. But as fallen human beings sharing this planet with other fallen human beings, we live under God's law of reciprocity—we reap what we sow. As Jesus says in the verse above, we receive what we give, both good and bad.

It is so easy to observe other people's lives and judge their motives and actions. Yet often we don't have the whole picture. And even if we did, who are we to judge and condemn? I once heard a story about a morbidly obese woman who bought a very small ice-cream cone from a vendor. The woman behind her made a cutting comment as she passed by with the cone, telling the large woman that if she would just exert some self-discipline, she would not be so fat. What the rude woman did not know was that the other woman had lost more than one hundred pounds the past year and allowed herself one small cone once a week as her only treat. We rarely know the whole story.

Most of us have heard the saying, "Do unto others as you would have them do unto you." In Matthew 7:12, Jesus put it this way: "In everything, do to others what you would have them do to you, for this sums up the Law and the Prophets." When we withhold judgment and condemnation of others, they will be withheld from us. Isn't that what we all want? If we are harsh and condemning of others, we will ultimately receive the same. On a positive note, being forgiving and generous will also be rewarded. The verse following our Scripture passage for today continues (as related to giving), "A good measure, pressed down, shaken together and running over, will be poured into your lap. For with the measure you use, it will be measured to you" (Luke 6:38).

God gives us more of what we give. If we give out of our abundance and goodness, he provides the means to continue the blessing to others. I have a sense—though it is not said directly—that we will also overflow with mercy and grace when we treat others as we wish to be treated.

Prayer

Heavenly Father, you see all and know all . . . and I do not. Please forgive me when I make judgments of people. I do not know the whole story of their lives. Help me to be your ambassador of mercy and grace. Help me to forgive and give as you empower me—and all this to your glory. Amen.

Worship

_____

_____

_____

Confession

_____

_____

_____

Thankfulness

_____

_____

_____

Prayer Requests

_____

_____

_____

- From the devotion above I have identified the lie I believe:

  _____

  _____

- The truth I now receive: _____

  _____

  _____

- I practiced healthy biblical self-talk today:
  ☐　　☐　　☐

- My key personal statement is:_____

  _____

  _____

- I have repeated that message at least three times today:
  ☐　　☐　　☐

- I have written my personal statement above or on an index card
  so I can continue to read it if I need renewal in this area.
  ☐

- Today I am learning to be more content and joyful by: ____

  _____

  _____

Day 37 Basking in the Light

But whoever lives by the truth comes into the light, so that it may be seen plainly that what he has done has been done through God.

John 3:21

Those of you who are over forty have probably noticed that you need good light to read small print these days. And if you are closer to fifty, you need good light and your reading glasses! An absence of light makes all the images on the page seem to run together and look like a blurry mess. Light illuminates and darkness hides. It is a simple principle that can also be applied to our hearts and minds.

Before we are exposed to the light of the gospel, we do not even realize we are living in darkness. But the gospel "is the power of God for the salvation of everyone who believes" (Rom. 1:16), and the moment its truth penetrates our heart, we are exposed to the most intense and penetrating light of truth. As believers we can embrace the light and live in a continually increasing awareness of God's love and power by becoming entrenched in his Word, or we can get distracted by life and turn away from the light and live in our own weakness rather than in his power.

As we studied earlier, walking by the Spirit and in the light is a moment-to-moment choice. If we choose to keep our focus on God, our mind in his Word, and our heart surrendered to his purposes, our life produces meaningful fruit that brings glory to him. Choosing to avoid the light of truth is an incredible waste. It is almost unfathomable to conceive why we would choose such a dark path when the light of truth is within our reach all the time. Turn your face toward the light of the Son. Follow his lead in the details of life. Then, what you do will bring glory to God and fill your heart with contentment.

> For you were once darkness, but now you are light in the Lord. Live as children of light (for the fruit of the light consists in all goodness, righteousness and truth) and find out what pleases the Lord.
>
> Ephesians 5:8–10

Prayer

Lord, please help me to consistently walk in the light of your truth. When life is going smoothly, I pray that I will crave your Word and intimacy with you as much as—even more than—when life is hard. Amen.

Worship

_____

_____

_____

Confession

_____

_____

_____

Thankfulness

_____

_____

_____

Prayer Requests

_____

_____

_____

- From the devotion above I have identified the lie I believe:

  _____

  _____

- The truth I now receive: _____

  _____

  _____

- I practiced healthy biblical self-talk today:
  ☐   ☐   ☐

- My key personal statement is:_____

  _____

  _____

- I have repeated that message at least three times today:
  ☐   ☐   ☐

- I have written my personal statement above or on an index card so I can continue to read it if I need renewal in this area. ☐

- Today I am learning to be more content and joyful by: ____

_____

_____

Day 38 Known by Love

A new command I give you: Love one another. As I have loved you, so you must love one another. All men will know that you are my disciples if you love one another.

John 13:34–35

Have you ever noticed a couple who has been married so long that you can barely tell the two people apart in their attitudes and mannerisms? They like the same food, activities, and even television shows. My grandmother and grandfather were like that. When my grandmother was diagnosed with multiple sclerosis in her mid-forties, you would have thought my grandfather had the disease because he was so sad and despondent for the first few years. He loved her so much that he could almost feel her pain, and he made it his mission to do everything he could to make her feel loved and comfortable. My parents have been married sixty years as of this writing, and they understand each other completely. They know what the other is going to say before it comes out of his or her mouth. You save a lot of time when you don't need to finish your sentences!

Christ wants his followers to be one—one with him as he is with the Father and one with each other. Do you sense a kindred spirit with every believer you know as members of the same family? A beautiful crimson cord ties us all together . . . the blood of Christ. While our personalities may not mesh and we may not understand each other in every way, we do understand that we are all sinners saved by grace who have the cure for the cancer of the human soul. That single truth should unite us in passion and purpose despite our differences.

We have a mission to share the good news of Christ's provision for sin with everyone who will listen. Without the unity of love reflecting his forgiveness, we look just like those still contaminated by sin. Why would people ever want what we have when they see us arguing, criticizing, and backbiting as we so often do? One of the easiest ways for the enemy to set us off course is to create division within the body of Christ. We become so busy with our own issues that we lose our joy and passion, bringing little glory to Christ.

This is not a new problem in the church. Paul wrote to early believers about this very thing, sometimes in kind words and sometimes with holy anger. He says in Colossians 3:12–14, "Therefore, as God's chosen people, holy and dearly loved, clothe yourselves with compassion, kindness, humility, gentleness and patience. Bear with each other and forgive whatever grievances you may have against one another. Forgive as the Lord forgave you. And over all these virtues put on love, which binds them all together in perfect unity."

Before we go out in the winter rain, sleet, wind, or snow, we always put on garments that protect us from the elements. In these verses, Paul tells us to "clothe ourselves" with the attitudes and actions that demonstrate to whom we belong. And then he says to "put on love." We don't wait to feel love and then act on it. We *put on* the actions, and then the feeling follows. When we are clothed with the apparel of Christ, we have a godly shield that protects us from the lies of the enemy and at the same time reflects the beauty of Christ's love to the lost. If you want to find deep joy and contentment in life, make it your purpose to dress yourself in Christ's love each day before you speak a word—even to yourself!

Prayer

Heavenly Father, please forgive me for wearing garments of criticism and harshness rather than love and grace some days. Gently remind me when I am doing this, and help me to clothe myself daily in your love and forgiveness so that they flow onto others. Amen.

Worship

_____

_____

_____

Confession

_____

_____

_____

Thankfulness

_____

_____

_____

Prayer Requests

_____

_____

_____

- From the devotion above I have identified the lie I believe:

  _____

  _____

- The truth I now receive: _____

  _____

  _____

- I practiced healthy biblical self-talk today:
  ☐   ☐   ☐

- My key personal statement is:_____

  _____

  _____

- I have repeated that message at least three times today:
  ☐   ☐   ☐

- I have written my personal statement above or on an index card so I can continue to read it if I need renewal in this area.
  ☐

- Today I am learning to be more content and joyful by: _____

_____

_____

Day 39 First Love

You have persevered and have endured hardships for my name, and
have not grown weary. Yet I hold this against you: You have forsaken
your first love. Remember the height from which you have fallen!
Repent and do the things you did at first. If you do not repent, I will
come to you and remove your lampstand from its place.

Revelation 2:3–5

Have you ever endured hardship for Christ? I can't say I really have.
I'm sure there are some people who knew me BC (before Christ) who
think I'm a religious nutcase. Perhaps I've offended some from the
platform when I share the gospel. But I can't say I've ever suffered for
my faith. If I ever do, I know I will be tested in a powerful way.

My friend Marilyn Williams just sent an email encouraging the
women in her life to pray for two women who are enduring great
hardship because of their faith.

> Two young Iranian Christian women are being held at the
> notorious Evin prison in Iran. They were arrested because
> of their Christian faith and have been accused of "anti-
> government" activity. They are in a cell with twenty-seven other
> women in terrible living conditions that have caused both to
> suffer ill health. They have not been allowed to see a doctor.
> However, they are very encouraged that Christians around the
> world are praying for them. They will be tried in court and
> face the possibility of being sentenced to life imprisonment. In

September 2008, the Iranian parliament passed the initial stages of a bill that would make apostasy (leaving Islam for another religion) a criminal offense, punishable by life imprisonment for women and death for men.

Imagine for a moment switching places with one of these women. She gets the opportunity to worship openly and freely at your church and fellowship with your friends. You are now sitting in a cold, dank cell praying that Christ will give you the strength to endure. You are frightened and hungry. Your only hope is that God will intervene supernaturally. Even in this fully surrendered state of imprisonment, Christ wants your utter devotion and love.

Sadly, for many of us, when the crisis is over, we often grow lukewarm in our passion for him. When my daughter Jamie was in prison, she said she finally understood what Mother Teresa meant when she said, "You don't know that Jesus is all you need until Jesus is all you have." Yet, Jamie is the first to admit that the minute she left her prison cell, the freedom and distractions took her mind off the Lord, and her first love did not always get his rightful first place.

Jesus tells the church at Ephesus that despite all the hardship they have endured, the lies they have rejected, and the good things they have done, he is most concerned that they have forsaken their first love. He is no longer their "one thing." Perhaps in defending their faith, they became more in love with the cause of Christ than Christ himself. However the change occurred, he demands repentance and a return to complete devotion. This very day, let us examine our hearts and ask ourselves if Christ is still on the throne of our lives—our all in all.

Prayer

Lord, I am so guilty of forsaking you in small and big ways each and every day. My needs, my comfort, my desires become the center of my focus until I am totally self-centered rather than Christ-centered. Please forgive me and guide me back to you, my first love. Amen.

Worship

_____

_____

_____

Confession

_____

_____

_____

Thankfulness

_____

_____

_____

Prayer Requests

_____

_____

_____

- From the devotion above I have identified the lie I believe:

  _____

  _____

- The truth I now receive: _____

  _____

  _____

- I practiced healthy biblical self-talk today:

  ☐   ☐   ☐

- My key personal statement is:_____

  _____

  _____

- I have repeated that message at least three times today:

  ☐   ☐   ☐

- I have written my personal statement above or on an index card so I can continue to read it if I need renewal in this area.

  ☐

- Today I am learning to be more content and joyful by: _____

  _____

  _____

Day 40 All of Me

Love the Lord your God with all your heart and with all your soul
and with all your mind and with all your strength.

Mark 12:30

If you've ever been deeply in love with anyone, you know that the
first weeks or months are consumed with thoughts of that person.
Your constant desire is to be with him and to please him. You remi-
nisce about your last moments together and look forward to your
next encounter. You are obsessed . . . in a good way!

Godliness, in essence, is an obsession with God. We can be obsessed with so many things—many of them of little value, some very
damaging. But being completely focused on God and his purposes
is the reason we exist. Unfortunately, our flesh is self-centered and
self-gratifying. It is only when we set our mind on things above
that we can walk in the Spirit and experience his incredible fruit. It
is in those moments that we have true peace. We sense that we are
safely nestled in the eye of the storm of life and that God is guiding,
loving, and protecting us.

Because we are easily distracted and imperfect human "doings,"
our desire to walk in the Spirit is often sidetracked because of the
cares of the world—our daily life. Striving to love God fully is a constant tug-of-war this side of heaven, but it is worth the effort. Pull
hard on your heart and mind as you refocus your thoughts on the
Lord moment to moment. God wants absolutely all of us, not just a
portion. Like a husband who is unwilling to share the intimacy of
his wife with another, God demands our entire heart. When we give
it to him, we experience a love so deep that it overflows to others in
the purest, most authentic form. Then we can build deep intimacy
with those who love us and great compassion for those who don't.

Understanding what God desires of us (actually commands us) is
the easy part. The Scripture passage for today was originally written
in the Old Testament book of Deuteronomy and was quoted by Jesus

and recorded in the Gospels. It is a common thread throughout the entire Bible. God wants us to love him with our entire being. The hard part is learning *how* to love him authentically and fully. To love someone with all of your heart, soul, mind, and strength, you must know that person intimately by spending time with him and sharing your heart as well. You can know God deeply by reading his love letter to us—the Bible. You can spend intimate time with him in prayer and practice his presence in your life. The Holy Spirit will testify that God is near and animate his Word in your life. Over time, you will grow in love and dependence on the only one who will never leave or forsake you.

We make time for what is most important to us. If our child becomes ill and must be rushed to the hospital, we drop everything and give her our total attention. All the cares of the world become small in comparison to the immediate situation. God wants that kind of attention from us all the time. It seems an impossible request, and it is. But with God *all* things are possible!

Prayer

Glorious God, to know that you actually desire my love is so amazing. I want to give you all of me and yet I fail so often because I put me first and you second. Please forgive me for my selfishness and draw me near. Help me love you in a way that honors you and puts you first. Amen.

Worship

_____

_____

_____

Confession

_____

_____

_____

Thankfulness

_____

_____

_____

Prayer Requests

_____

_____

_____

- From the devotion above I have identified the lie I believe:

  _____

  _____

- The truth I now receive: _____

  _____

  _____

- I practiced healthy biblical self-talk today:
  ☐   ☐   ☐

- My key personal statement is:_____

  _____

  _____

- I have repeated that message at least three times today:
  ☐ ☐ ☐

- I have written my personal statement above or on an index card
  so I can continue to read it if I need renewal in this area.
  ☐

- Today I am learning to be more content and joyful by: _____

  _____

  _____

Have you ever asked yourself any of these questions?

Why do I exist?
Does my life have purpose?
Does God even know or care about me?

The answers to those questions make a huge difference in how you perceive and ultimately live your life. You exist because God chose to give you life. He has a universal and specific purpose for your life. His universal purpose for every single person that has ever been born is that we have a personal, intimate relationship with him. His specific purpose is that once we know him that we share his love with others both in sharing the truth of his Word—the Bible—and by reaching out in tangible, practical ways. He cares deeply about each of us—so much that he says that he knows the number of hairs on our head!

If you are not absolutely sure that you have an intimate relationship with God through the blood of his Son, Jesus Christ, it is my prayer that you have come to see a glimpse of him in these pages and have begun to understand that he loves you personally and intimately. To do that, you need to know a few simple facts.

Often our concept of God and his expectations are muddled because we do not think as God thinks. We tend to believe that life is graded on a curve and if you do more "good" things than "bad" things, God is obligated to accept you. The Bible (God's love letter to us) tells us exactly what God thinks and expects. It tells us that God is perfect and holy and that he cannot relate to us in our sinful state. In Romans 3:23 it says, "All have sinned and fall short of the glory of God." That includes those who appear "super-spiritual" like Billy Graham. Like us, he also falls short. In Romans 6:23, it says: "The wages of sin is death." That means death to our souls and ultimately permanent separation from God.

It would seem at first glance that God's desire to have relationship with us and our sin (rebellion from God by living for ourselves rather than him) is an unsolvable dilemma. However, God knew before he created the first humans (with free wills) that we would sin. He had the problem covered as expressed in one of the most well-known Bible verses, John 3:16: "For God so loved the world that he gave his one and only Son, that whoever believes in him shall not perish but have eternal life."

Jesus Christ came to the earth in the body of a man for the sole purpose of dying for our sins . . . for your sins. If you were the only person alive, he would have done that just for you. If you believe that fact and accept his free gift of forgiveness, you will be saved and have eternal life. It's that simple.

You don't have to pray a formal prayer, walk down an aisle, or perform some ritual to accept Jesus as your Savior. You simply need to *believe* that he died for your sins and paid the penalty in full. If you are seeking God but unsure what you believe, I encourage you to pray for him to reveal himself to you and to help you with any disbelief. In Jeremiah 29:13 it says, "You will seek me and find me when you seek me with all your heart." God is not playing a game of spiritual hide and seek with you. He wants you to understand truth and believe. It is in our humility, when we come to the end of ourselves and realize we are not the master of our fate—but God is—that he meets you.

One of the wonderful things about believing in Jesus Christ is that he gives you direct access to God through prayers. While a prayer does not "save" you, it does communicate your heart to God and help confirm your belief that Jesus died for your sins and secured a place in heaven for you. You can tell God in your own words, or with a simple prayer like this one below.

Heavenly Father, thank you for drawing me to you and showing me that Jesus is "the way, the truth and the life" and that "no one comes to you except through him." I believe that Jesus died for my sins—past, present, and even future—and I pray that through his blood you will forgive me for all my sins. Help me to follow you, learn more about you, and love you with all my heart, soul, mind, and strength. Amen.

Notes

Chapter 1 Expectations and Your Misery Factor

1. Timothy R. Scott, Ph.D., pastor, Grace Church San Diego, San Diego, CA. Tim can be reached at www.gracesd.com.

Chapter 2 The Balancing Act

1. Oswald Chambers, *My Utmost for His Highest* (Grand Rapids: Discovery House Publishers, 1963), 337.
2. F. B. Meyer, *Meditations on the Sermon on the Mount* (Wheaton, IL: Victor Books, 1995), 35.
3. Dr. Richard Swenson, *Margin* (Colorado Springs: NavPress, 1992), 13.
4. Edwin Louis Cole, *Profiles in Courageous Manhood* (Tulsa: Albury, 1998), 25.

Chapter 3 Life's Defining Habits

1. Dr. Archibald D. Hart, *Habits of the Mind* (Wheaton: Tyndale, 1996), 4–5.
2. Ibid., 6.

Chapter 4 The Cancer of Discontentment

1. Charles Spurgeon, *2,200 Quotations from the Writings of Charles A. Spurgeon* (Grand Rapids: Baker, 1988), 41.
2. I asked my pastor, Tim Scott, whom I've quoted several times in this book, for a book recommendation related to divorce. His recommendation is George Ewald, *Jesus and Divorce: A Biblical Guide for Ministry to Divorced Persons* (Scottdale, PA: Herald Press, 1991).

3. Drew Josephs, *The Top 100 Men of the Bible* (Uhrichsville, OH: Barbour Publishing, 2008), 47.

4. Ibid., 46.

Chapter 5 The Secret of Contentment

1. Hart, *Habits of the Mind*, 148.

2. Ibid., 149.

3. Charles Ryrie, *Ryrie Study Bible* (Chicago: Moody, 1995), 2063–64.

4. Ibid., 1883.

5. Danna Demetre, *Change Your Habits, Change Your Life*, 59.

6. Ibid., 60.

7. Ryrie, *Ryrie Study Bible*, 1873.

8. Brennan Manning, *Ruthless Trust: The Ragamuffin's Path to God* (New York: HarperCollins, 2000), 94.

Chapter 6 Walk a Mile in My Pumps

1. Mary James, recording artist and speaker, can be contacted at www.mary-james.com.

2. Sylvia Lange, recording artist and speaker, can be contacted at www.sylvialange.com.

3. Diana Twadell can be contacted at dianainsd@yahoo.com.

4. Kris Peterson can be contacted at KristanRae@aol.com.

5. Kimberly Scott can be contacted at kimberly@gracesd.com.

6. Marilyn Williams can be contacted at marilynsministry@cox.net.

Chapter 7 The Forty-Day Journey to Rediscover Contentment and Joy

1. Louie Giglio, *The Air I Breathe* (Sisters, OR: Multnomah, 2003), 10–11.

2. Manning, *Ruthless Trust*, 3.

3. C. S. Lewis, *The Quotable Lewis*, ed. Wayne Martindale and Jerry Root (Wheaton: Tyndale, 1989), 484.

4. Manning, *Ruthless Trust*, 102–3.

Day 10 In Jesus's Name

1. Greg Koukl, *Stand to Reason* website, www.str.org.

Day 14 God Provides

1. Chambers, *My Utmost for His Highest*, 131.

2. Elbert Hubbard, www.thinkexist.com.

Day 20 Heavenly Inventory

1. Randy Alcorn, *Heaven* (Wheaton: Tyndale, 2004), 470.

Day 21 What's in It for *Me*?

1. Alcorn, *Heaven*, 47, 325, 470.

Day 34 Everything

1. Randy Alcorn, *Money, Possessions, and Eternity* (Wheaton: Tyndale, 2003), 44.

Day 35 Where Is Your Treasure?

1. Manning, *Ruthless Trust*, 24.

Recommended Resources

Many life circumstances are out of our control. But we do have control over how we choose to interpret them and the actions we take. As you continue on your journey toward greater passion, purpose, and joy, I encourage you to develop some lifelong habits that will serve you well when trials and tribulations—or just plain stress—come your way.

First, make an appointment with the King every day and read his love letter—the Bible—every chance you get. As Kay Arthur said so wisely in her endorsement of this book, "Make sure that no devotional, no book, keeps you from studying God's book—the Bible—for yourself." His living and active Word can work in us personally only when we have filled ourselves to overflowing with it.

Second, give yourself the same grace God gives you in the journey toward becoming the person he designed you to be. You are a work in progress—we all are. Be patient. As you reset your mind on things above and practice the tools I've shared in this book, you will become transformed by the renewing of your mind.

It is a great privilege to share my teaching with you. I count it an honor that you've read to the last page! As a thank you, I want to offer you a special reader discount. If you choose to order anything and use the code WHTML, you will receive a 10 percent discount on all my resources until January 2012. These resources include the books and CDs listed below. Visit my website at www. dannademetre.com.

May God bless your efforts as you set your mind on things above and submit to the transforming power of his Word.

Danna

What Happened to My Life? Healthy Self-Talk CD
Change Your Habits, Change Your Life book
Change Your Habits, Change Your Life Healthy Self-Talk CD
Scale Down book
Scale Down workbook
Scale Down Healthy Self-Talk CD
Scale Down . . . Live It Up CD series (6 sessions)
Scale Down . . . Live It Up DVD series (6 sessions)

Self-described as a work in progress, **Danna Demetre** has learned how to find deep satisfaction by putting first things first in each area of her life. A survivor of marital infidelity, the heartbreak of rebellious children, the paralysis of unrelenting panic attacks, and prolonged bondage to food, she has personally discovered that God's Word is truly living and active and more powerful than a two-edged sword (Heb. 4:12). In addition to over twenty-five years in the health and fitness industries, Danna is a former radio talk show host and continues to be a sought-after media guest. She is a popular international speaker and author of several books, including *Scale Down* with its companion church curriculum, and *Change Your Habits, Change Your Life*. Danna lives in San Diego with her husband, Lew, and their thirteen-year-old, Jesse. For more information, visit www. DannaDemetre.com.

Change is possible!

Embark on a 40-day journey to permanent change in your life and toward being the person God designed you to be.

Meet Danna at www.dannademetre.com